MAYER SMITH

A Spell Between Shadows and Desire

Copyright © 2025 by Mayer Smith

All rights reserved. No part of this publication may be reproduced, stored or transmitted in any form or by any means, electronic, mechanical, photocopying, recording, scanning, or otherwise without written permission from the publisher. It is illegal to copy this book, post it to a website, or distribute it by any other means without permission.

This novel is entirely a work of fiction. The names, characters and incidents portrayed in it are the work of the author's imagination. Any resemblance to actual persons, living or dead, events or localities is entirely coincidental.

Mayer Smith asserts the moral right to be identified as the author of this work.

Mayer Smith has no responsibility for the persistence or accuracy of URLs for external or third-party Internet Websites referred to in this publication and does not guarantee that any content on such Websites is, or will remain, accurate or appropriate.

Designations used by companies to distinguish their products are often claimed as trademarks. All brand names and product names used in this book and on its cover are trade names, service marks, trademarks and registered trademarks of their respective owners. The publishers and the book are not associated with any product or vendor mentioned in this book. None of the companies referenced within the book have endorsed the book.

First edition

*This book was professionally typeset on Reedsy.
Find out more at reedsy.com*

Contents

1	A Sorceress on the Run	1
2	The Cursed Blade	8
3	A Deal with Darkness	15
4	Secrets in the Blood	22
5	The Empire's War Machine	31
6	A Kiss of Power	39
7	The Assassin's Nightmare	49
8	The City of Lost Magic	57
9	Dancing on the Edge of Desire	65
10	Betrayal Under Moonlight	72
11	A Curse That Binds Two Souls	80
12	The Emperor's Deception	88
13	A Kingdom of Shadows	95
14	The Last Sanctuary	102
15	A Desperate Bargain	109
16	The Assassin's Heart	117
17	A Spell Between Shadows and Desire	124
18	The Fall of an Empire	131
19	A Love That Defies Fate	138
20	Whispers Beyond the Veil	144

One

A Sorceress on the Run

The stench of burnt flesh and charred wood still clung to Althea's cloak as she sprinted through the labyrinthine alleys of Valcoris. The city, bathed in the eerie glow of the burning marketplace behind her, pulsed with the frantic cries of merchants and soldiers alike. Her lungs burned from the acrid smoke, but she didn't stop. She couldn't stop.

Behind her, the clang of armored boots on stone sent ice through her veins.

"There! The sorceress! Don't let her escape!"

The Order of the Crimson Brand was relentless. They always were. They had hunted her across three provinces, forced her into the shadows like a common thief, and now—now they had nearly trapped her.

A Spell Between Shadows and Desire

A spell fizzled at her fingertips as she ducked into an abandoned courtyard, pressing herself against the cold brick of a crumbling wall. Her magic was erratic, drained from the last desperate burst she had unleashed to keep them at bay. She had never meant to burn the market, but panic had a way of making the flames greedy.

A hush settled over the city block. The pursuers had paused. Listening.

Althea dared to peek around the corner. The street was too open, too exposed. The moon hung above like a watchful god, silver light gleaming off the soldiers' plated armor as they fanned out. The sigil of the empire—a serpent coiled around a dagger—was emblazoned on their chests, marking them as imperial enforcers.

Her fingers clenched into fists. She was no fool. If they caught her, they wouldn't just kill her.

They would make an example of her.

Footsteps approached. Slow, measured.

Althea flattened herself against the wall, heart pounding so violently she feared they would hear it. She had to move.

A wooden balcony loomed overhead, its support beams rotten but still sturdy enough to climb. She reached for the nearest ledge, her muscles screaming in protest as she pulled herself up. Her legs ached, her arms trembled, but she forced herself to move. The fabric of her cloak snagged on splintered wood as she scrambled over the railing and into the upper floor of a long-abandoned tailor's shop.

Cobwebs clung to the ruined shelves. Motes of dust swirled in the moonlight, disturbed by her ragged breaths. Below, the soldiers barked orders.

"She couldn't have gone far."

Althea moved swiftly but silently, weaving through the debris toward the window on the far side. She had escaped countless times before, and she would do so again.

But as she reached the window, she froze.

A man stood in the alley below.

Not a soldier. Not a merchant or a hapless citizen caught in the chaos.

He was draped in black, his silhouette blending seamlessly with the shadows cast by the flickering streetlamps. A long blade rested at his hip, its silvered edge catching the light in a way that made her stomach twist. His presence was unnatural—too still, too patient.

Althea knew killers when she saw them.

She sucked in a sharp breath, stepping back into the darkness of the shop's interior.

Her pulse roared in her ears. Was he waiting for her? Had someone else sent him?

The soldiers moved on, their footsteps fading into the distance. She should have been relieved, but the weight of unseen eyes pressed against her skin. Slowly, carefully, she eased back toward the window, peering out once more.

The alley was empty.

She exhaled, shoulders dropping an inch, but unease still curled in her stomach like a viper. She had lived too long in the shadows to ignore the feeling of being watched.

There was no time to waste.

She pushed open the window and climbed onto the tiled rooftop, keeping low as she moved. The city stretched before her in a labyrinth of narrow streets and towering spires, the river that divided the capital gleaming under the moonlight. If she could reach the bridge, she could disappear into the lower district before sunrise.

A whisper of movement.

Her instincts screamed.

She spun just as the figure from the alley appeared, stepping onto the rooftop as if the laws of physics did not apply to him.

He moved with the grace of a predator, each step precise, each motion deliberate.

Althea's breath hitched.

The assassin.

Her fingers flexed at her sides, searching for a spark of magic, but the well inside her was still drained. She took a step back, gauging the distance between herself and the next rooftop.

"Run, and I'll catch you," the man said, his voice smooth as silk but edged with steel.

Althea swallowed hard, her mind racing.

She had spent years running.

Tonight, she would fight.

She lunged.

He was faster.

A blur of movement—his hand caught her wrist, twisting it effortlessly behind her back. She gasped at the sudden pain, twisting against his hold. He smelled of steel and rain, and his grip was unyielding.

"You have quite the reputation," he murmured against her ear. "A rogue sorceress. A danger to the empire."

She gritted her teeth. "And you are?"

He chuckled, the sound devoid of amusement. "Someone you should fear."

With a sharp yank, she freed her wrist and spun, driving her knee toward his stomach. He dodged easily, sidestepping with an elegance that set her on edge.

Althea reached for the dagger hidden in her boot, but the assassin was already a step ahead. In one fluid motion, he twisted her arm, forcing her to drop the weapon. The blade clattered to the rooftop, useless.

Panic clawed at her throat.

"I don't make a habit of killing unarmed women," he said, watching her carefully. "But if you force my hand, I won't hesitate."

Althea's jaw clenched.

She had one last option.

Drawing in a deep breath, she let the remnants of her magic flare to life. A single ember, a whisper of fire, curled at her fingertips. She barely had enough energy left to summon it, but it would have to be enough.

The assassin's eyes darkened.

"Ah," he said, as if he had expected this. "Magic."

Althea lunged again, this time aiming the fire at his chest. But as the flame leapt toward him, he moved—faster than she thought possible.

And then, suddenly, he was behind her.

A sharp pain at her throat. The cold press of steel.

The fire flickered and died.

Althea stilled, her pulse hammering against the blade.

"I warned you," the assassin said softly. "Now, you're coming with me."

The shadows of Valcoris stretched long and dark around them, swallowing the city whole.

Two

The Cursed Blade

The blade at Althea's throat was cold—unnervingly so, as if it had been forged from the very essence of the void. She dared not swallow, dared not move. Every breath she took threatened to press her skin further against the razor's edge. The assassin's grip was steady, his body impossibly still behind her, as though he were carved from stone.

"You're making a mistake," she whispered.

His voice was close, too close. "I don't make mistakes."

The metal bit into her skin just enough to draw the smallest drop of blood. A silent warning.

Althea's mind raced. This wasn't the first time she had stared death in the face, but something about this man felt different.

The Cursed Blade

Assassins usually reveled in their kills, playing with their prey, waiting for the fear to settle in before the final strike. But this one? There was no mockery in his tone, no sadistic pleasure in his hold—just grim certainty, as though he had already seen the outcome of their encounter.

Which meant he thought she was already dead.

She refused to accept that.

In one swift motion, she yanked her knee up and back, aiming for his ribs. The force of her movement threw them both off balance. He hissed, but his grip tightened before she could slip away.

The blade left her throat, only to return in a flash of silver.

Althea ducked just in time. The weapon sliced through the air where her neck had been a heartbeat before. A killing blow. He hadn't been toying with her. He had meant to end it right there.

Her instincts screamed at her to run, but she ignored them.

Instead, she lunged.

Her hands grasped for his wrist, trying to wrench the dagger from his grip, but his strength was unnatural. His body twisted, redirecting her momentum, and before she knew it, she was being thrown.

Her back hit the tiled roof hard. The impact knocked the air from her lungs. The assassin was on her in an instant, pressing the blade's flat against her sternum, pinning her down.

Althea barely had time to register the way his eyes flickered—like a storm barely held at bay.

Then she felt it.

A pulse of something dark.

The dagger in his hand trembled, almost as if it had a mind of its own. Shadows curled from its hilt, slithering through the air like tendrils of smoke. The sight sent a bolt of unease through her. This wasn't an ordinary weapon.

It was cursed.

Her breath hitched as realization sank in.

"You're bound to it," she murmured, eyes darting to his knuckles, the way they clenched tighter, as if fighting an unseen force. "You can't let go, can you?"

His jaw tensed. For the first time, something flickered across his face—an emotion she couldn't quite place.

Then, just as quickly as it appeared, it was gone.

He pressed the blade harder against her. "Stop talking."

The air between them was electric. Every muscle in her body screamed at her to move, to do something, but she forced herself to stay still. He had the advantage. If she tried to use magic now, drained as she was, she would fail.

And failure meant death.

Instead, she studied him.

His face was angular, sharp in the way of a man who had known too much hardship. A shadow of stubble traced his jaw, and a thin scar ran from his temple down to his cheekbone. His eyes—gods, his eyes—were the color of dark steel, unreadable, yet brimming with something dangerous.

"How long has it been?" she asked softly.

His brow furrowed. "What?"

"Since the curse took hold of you."

Something in his expression cracked for the briefest second.

Althea had been right.

She wasn't sure how, but she knew the signs of cursed magic when she saw them. The way his fingers twitched involuntarily, how his breath hitched when the dagger pulsed with that strange energy—it wasn't natural.

"You're no ordinary assassin," she continued, her voice barely above a whisper. "Someone did this to you. Someone bound you to that blade."

His silence was confirmation enough.

Althea swallowed hard. If he truly had no control over the weapon, then killing her might not be his choice at all. That meant there was a way to break the hold it had on him.

And that meant she could use it.

Slowly, deliberately, she reached up and pressed her fingertips to the dagger's hilt.

The reaction was instant.

A sharp crackle filled the air, like a thousand whispers shrieking at once. The assassin jerked back as if burned, his grip on the blade faltering for the first time.

Althea seized her chance.

She rolled to the side, kicking her leg out and sweeping him off balance. He staggered, but before he could recover, she was already scrambling to her feet. Her magic flared, raw and untamed, and she thrust her hand out.

Flames erupted from her palm.

The assassin barely managed to dodge. The fire singed the edge of his cloak as he leapt back, but he didn't fall. Instead, he

The Cursed Blade

skidded to a stop, breathing heavily, his gaze locked onto her like a predator tracking its prey.

Althea could still feel the echo of whatever dark magic clung to that blade. It wasn't just an enchanted weapon—it was alive in some way.

And it wanted blood.

The assassin straightened, rolling his shoulders as if shaking off the lingering effect of her touch. His expression was unreadable, but his grip on the dagger was firm again.

"I should kill you," he said.

She smirked despite herself. "You already tried."

Something that might have been amusement flickered across his face, but it was gone just as quickly.

"I have orders," he said. "You come with me. Or you die."

Althea exhaled slowly, weighing her options. She couldn't outrun him, not indefinitely. And if he really was bound to that cursed blade, she might be the only one who could break the spell.

Which meant she needed him as much as he needed her.

So she did the only thing she could.

She raised her hands in mock surrender and took a step toward him. "Fine. Take me."

His eyes narrowed, suspicious.

"But," she added, tilting her head, "I'm not some helpless girl you can chain and drag to your masters." She met his gaze, unflinching. "I'm coming willingly. And that means we do this on my terms."

He let out a short, humorless laugh. "You think you have terms?"

"I think you don't have a choice."

She gestured toward the dagger in his hand, where the shadows still pulsed hungrily.

"You need me," she said, watching his expression carefully. "And I think we both know it."

A long silence stretched between them. Then, finally, he lowered the blade.

"Then let's see how long you survive," he murmured.

Althea smiled. "Try to keep up."

The night around them was thick with shadows, but as they disappeared into the depths of Valcoris, Althea couldn't shake the feeling that this was only the beginning.

Three

A Deal with Darkness

T he night had swallowed them whole.

The winding alleyways of Valcoris stretched like veins through the dying city, filled with the scent of damp stone and rot. Arelan moved like a shadow ahead of Althea, his every step controlled, deliberate. She followed, though every instinct in her body warned against it. He was an assassin bound to a cursed blade, a hunter who had already tried to end her once. And yet, here she was—walking willingly into the depths of whatever abyss he intended to lead her.

Althea didn't fool herself into thinking this was trust. No, this was survival.

She kept her steps light, her fingers twitching at her sides as she tried to summon her magic. A weak flicker of warmth sparked at her fingertips, but it was sluggish, unsteady. She had drained too much energy in the escape, and now her power was little more than a whisper.

She needed time to recover. She needed a plan.

Arelan took a sharp turn down a narrow passage, his voice cutting through the silence.

"Keep up."

Althea scowled but didn't argue. She glanced up at the sliver of sky visible between the rooftops. The moon hung low, a cold and distant eye. The city was quieter now—no more cries of merchants, no more soldiers barking orders. But that didn't mean it was safe.

Arelan stopped abruptly in front of a rusted iron door set into the side of a decrepit building. He rapped his knuckles against the metal in a precise rhythm—three short knocks, a pause, then two more.

Althea tensed. "Where are we?"

Arelan didn't answer.

The door groaned open a moment later, revealing a man with sunken eyes and a jagged scar cutting across his lip. He peered at Arelan, then at Althea, his gaze calculating.

"She's with me," Arelan said.

A Deal with Darkness

The man grunted and stepped aside. "Your funeral."

The moment they entered, the door slammed shut behind them, cutting off the outside world.

The air inside was thick—heavy with the scent of damp wood, burnt herbs, and something metallic beneath it all. The room was dimly lit by a cluster of candles dripping wax onto a scarred wooden table. Shelves lined the walls, cluttered with vials, books, and objects Althea didn't dare look at too closely. A faint hum filled the air, the unmistakable pulse of magic.

Arelan strode forward without hesitation. "I need it removed."

The figure sitting at the far end of the room lifted his head.

Althea's breath caught.

The man was old—far older than he should have been, his skin withered like parchment, his eyes an unnatural shade of red. He was draped in a cloak that shimmered unnaturally, as though the fabric refused to settle into one color. The very air around him seemed to shift, bending the light.

A sorcerer. A powerful one.

The old man's gaze flickered to the dagger at Arelan's hip.

"Ah," he murmured, his voice a rasp. "The cursed blade."

Althea felt Arelan stiffen beside her.

The sorcerer's lips curled into something that was neither a smile nor a sneer. "Still bound to you, is it? Tighter than ever?"

Arelan's jaw clenched. "Can you remove it?"

The sorcerer leaned forward, resting his bony hands on the table. "That depends. Are you willing to pay the price?"

Arelan hesitated, and in that pause, Althea saw something rare—uncertainty.

She stepped forward. "What kind of price?"

The sorcerer's gaze slid to her, eyes gleaming with interest. "Ah. The sorceress. I was wondering when you'd speak."

Althea ignored the chill that ran down her spine. "Answer the question."

The old man chuckled, a dry, brittle sound. "The dagger isn't merely cursed. It's bound to his soul. To sever that connection..." He tilted his head, studying Arelan. "It would require a trade."

Arelan's hands curled into fists. "What kind of trade?"

The sorcerer's smile widened. "A life."

Silence.

The air between them thickened, charged with something

unseen.

Althea looked at Arelan, trying to gauge his reaction, but his face was unreadable.

A life.

She didn't need to ask whose.

Arelan exhaled slowly, then reached for the dagger. The moment his fingers brushed the hilt, the air around them shifted. A pulse of dark energy rippled outward, strong enough to make the candles flicker. The sorcerer's expression darkened.

"This blade," he murmured, "it was forged in the depths of a dying star. The one who created it… did not intend for it to be removed."

Althea watched as the shadows coiled around Arelan's hand, crawling up his arm like living things. He didn't flinch.

She turned back to the sorcerer. "There has to be another way."

The old man's gaze sharpened. "There is."

Arelan's head snapped up. "What?"

The sorcerer's fingers drummed against the table. "The empire has its own secrets. Deep beneath the capital, hidden in the ruins of the first kingdom, there lies an artifact—a relic of the old gods. It is said to sever all bonds, even those tied to the soul."

Althea narrowed her eyes. "And you want it."

The sorcerer's smile was all teeth.

Arelan let out a slow breath. "That's the deal, then. We bring you the artifact, and you free me from the dagger."

The old man nodded. "That is the deal."

Althea didn't like it. She didn't trust it. But what choice did they have?

Arelan turned to her. "You don't have to do this."

She held his gaze. "Neither do you."

A beat of silence stretched between them.

Then Arelan nodded.

Althea turned back to the sorcerer. "Where do we find it?"

The old man's smile deepened, and for the first time, Althea felt truly afraid.

"Beneath the emperor's throne," he said.

The weight of the words settled over them like a storm cloud.

A Deal with Darkness

Stealing from the empire was one thing.

Breaking into the heart of its power?

That was suicide.

And yet, as she looked at Arelan—the assassin with a cursed blade, a man who should have been her enemy—she knew she wasn't going to turn back.

She had made her choice.

The deal had been struck.

Now, there was no going back.

Four

Secrets in the Blood

The scent of damp stone and aged parchment filled the air as Althea and Arelan navigated the underbelly of Valcoris. The old tunnels beneath the city stretched in endless darkness, twisting and curling beneath the empire's streets like the veins of a dying beast. Torchlight flickered against the slick stone walls, casting their elongated shadows into distorted figures that danced with every step.

Althea's fingers twitched at her sides, instinctively reaching for her magic. It had been hours since they left the sorcerer's den, and yet the weight of his words clung to her like a curse. The relic they sought lay beneath the emperor's throne. An impossible task.

And yet, it was the only way to break Arelan's bond to that blade.

She stole a glance at him as they walked. He was quiet—too quiet. Arelan had always carried himself with a detached precision, but tonight there was something else in his movements. Something slower, heavier. The dagger at his hip pulsed like a heartbeat, as though it had a mind of its own.

The silence stretched between them until Althea couldn't take it anymore.

"What aren't you telling me?"

Arelan didn't stop walking. His gaze remained fixed ahead, scanning the darkness. "You'll have to be more specific."

She clenched her jaw. "The blade. The curse. The way that sorcerer looked at you like he already knew what was wrong."

A muscle in his jaw ticked.

"That's not important right now."

Althea let out a humorless laugh. "Not important? You're bound to a weapon that drains your soul every time you use it, and you don't think I should be worried?"

Arelan exhaled through his nose. "Worrying won't change anything."

His refusal to speak only made her more determined.

She reached for his wrist before she could think better of it, stopping him mid-step. The moment their skin met, a jolt shot through her—sharp, cold, like ice shattering in her veins.

She gasped.

Images flooded her mind. A battlefield under a blood-red sky. A younger Arelan, his face streaked with soot and blood, kneeling before a figure cloaked in darkness. The dagger gleamed in his hands, its edge slick with fresh death.

A voice, deep and ancient, echoed through her skull.

This blade will never leave you. Until the debt is paid. Until the last drop of your blood has been given.

Althea yanked her hand back as if burned. The vision dissolved, leaving her breathless and shaken.

Arelan stared at her, his expression unreadable.

"What the hell was that?" she whispered.

His eyes darkened. "You saw it."

Althea swallowed. "Not everything. But enough."

His gaze flickered, unreadable, before he turned away. "It doesn't matter."

She grabbed his arm again—this time more forcefully. "Stop saying that."

Arelan's entire body tensed, but he didn't pull away. The air between them was thick, charged with something neither of them wanted to acknowledge.

Althea took a breath, steadying herself. "That dagger isn't just cursed, Arelan. It's bonded to your blood. The sorcerer said it was tied to your soul, but it's more than that, isn't it? It's feeding off you."

His lips pressed into a thin line.

She exhaled. "How long?"

Arelan hesitated. Then—so quietly she almost didn't hear it—he answered.

"Ten years."

Althea's chest tightened.

Ten years.

He had been carrying this burden for a decade. Every kill, every life taken, feeding something dark, something ancient. She had seen it in the vision—how the blade had been placed in his hands, how the words of that unknown figure had sealed his fate.

She suddenly understood why he was so desperate to be rid of it.

Her voice was softer this time. "Who did this to you?"

Arelan's gaze flicked away. "It doesn't matter."

"You keep saying that, but it does." She stepped closer, lowering her voice. "Who gave you the dagger, Arelan?"

A long pause.

Then, finally, he met her eyes.

"The emperor."

A cold chill ran down her spine.

Althea barely managed to keep her expression neutral, but inside, her mind was reeling. The emperor himself had given Arelan this blade? That changed everything. If the relic they sought lay beneath his throne, then this wasn't just about stealing an artifact anymore.

This was about unraveling something far greater.

Arelan must have sensed her thoughts, because his voice turned sharp. "You don't need to get involved in this."

Althea let out a short, humorless laugh. "Too late."

He sighed. "Althea—"

A sudden shuffling noise cut him off.

Both of them snapped to attention.

Althea's magic flared at her fingertips as Arelan's hand dropped to his dagger. The shadows around them stretched and curled, distorting unnaturally.

They weren't alone.

The air grew thick, suffocating. A whispering sound slithered through the tunnel, brushing against the edges of her mind like a clawed hand.

Then—

A figure lunged from the darkness.

Althea barely had time to react before she was shoved back, her magic bursting from her hands in an uncontrolled surge. Fire erupted, illuminating the tunnel for a brief second, and she caught a glimpse of their attacker.

Not a soldier.

Not a man.

Its skin was ashen, its eyes hollow pits of black, its mouth twisted into a grotesque grin. Ancient runes glowed along its body, shifting like living ink.

A revenant.

Althea's stomach dropped.

Revenants were the empire's darkest secret—warriors resurrected from death, their souls trapped between worlds, bound by magic older than the kingdom itself.

The creature hissed, lunging again.

Arelan moved first.

His blade sliced through the air with deadly precision, but the moment it connected with the revenant's flesh, the runes along its body pulsed—absorbing the strike like water swallowing a stone.

Althea cursed. "Magic-resistant. Of course it is."

The revenant twisted, its jagged claws swiping toward Arelan's chest. He dodged, but not fast enough. The creature's talons raked across his arm, black smoke curling from the wound.

Arelan hissed in pain, but he didn't stop. He shifted his stance, drawing the cursed dagger in a reverse grip. This time, when he struck, the blade pulsed—shadows curling around it like living things.

The revenant froze.

Arelan drove the dagger deep into its chest.

A guttural, inhuman shriek filled the tunnel, and the creature convulsed violently. The runes along its body flickered—once, twice—before dimming completely.

Then, with one final shudder, it collapsed into dust.

Silence.

Arelan staggered back, breathing heavily.

Althea rushed to his side, grabbing his arm. His wound was worse than she had thought—the black smoke curling from his skin wasn't just residue from the creature.

It was something deeper.

Something darker.

Althea pressed her palm against the wound, ignoring Arelan's protest. A faint glow spread from her fingertips as she reached for whatever magic she had left.

The moment her magic touched his blood, she felt it.

Darkness.

It coiled beneath his skin like a second soul, something unnatural and ancient. Something that didn't belong to him.

She looked up, heart pounding.

This wasn't just a curse.

Arelan's very blood had been altered.

And whoever had done it—whoever had bound him to that blade—had ensured that he would never truly be free.

Not unless they found that relic.

Not unless they broke the emperor's hold over him.

Althea met Arelan's gaze, her pulse thundering in her ears.

"We need to move," she whispered.

Arelan clenched his jaw, nodding.

Neither of them spoke of what she had just discovered.

But they both knew the truth.

Arelan's fate was far worse than either of them had realized.

Five

The Empire's War Machine

The empire was awake.

The clang of iron boots against cobblestone echoed through the narrow streets as the imperial forces moved ruthlessly. Althea crouched in the shadows of an abandoned wine cellar, her breath shallow, her pulse thrumming like a war drum. She could see the soldiers march past through a crack in the wooden slats, their crimson banners trailing behind them like the tongues of hungry flames.

They were searching.

For her.

For Arelan.

The encounter with the revenant had rattled her more than she cared to admit. It had not been a mindless beast. No, it had been something far worse—an engineered abomination of flesh and magic, created to obey without question. The empire had always dabbled in forbidden sorcery, but this was proof that they had mastered it.

And that meant they had grown far more dangerous than she had imagined.

She turned her gaze toward Arelan, leaning against the damp stone wall, his face paler than before. His wounded arm was wrapped in a torn strip of fabric, but the black veins beneath his skin still pulsed, an ominous reminder of the darkness eating away at him.

"How bad is it?" she whispered.

Arelan exhaled through his nose. "I've had worse."

Althea didn't believe him. The magic inside his blood was changing, mutating. She had seen it in how his fingers twitched when he gripped the dagger and how his breaths came faster than they should.

"You should have let me heal it properly," she murmured.

Arelan glanced at her, his expression unreadable. "It's not something your magic can heal."

She hated that he was right.

The Empire's War Machine

A distant horn blast shattered the quiet, followed by marching—hundreds, maybe thousands, of soldiers moving through the city.

Althea felt a chill creep down her spine.

That wasn't a search party.

That was an army.

She rose carefully, peeking through the gap in the wooden slats. The soldiers had stopped at the city's central square, where the towering iron gates of the Arx Caelum stood. The imperial fortress loomed over Valcoris like an unyielding giant, its spires stabbing into the sky like a warning to all who dared defy the empire's rule.

Althea's hands tightened into fists.

That was where they needed to go.

Alan followed her gaze, his expression darkening. "You think the artifact is inside?"

She nodded. "The emperor wouldn't keep something that powerful anywhere else."

Arelan's jaw tightened. "Then we have a problem."

Althea frowned. "More than the usual ones?"

A Spell Between Shadows and Desire

Arelan gestured toward the gathering army. "That isn't just any division of soldiers. Those are the Imperium Forged."

She inhaled sharply.

The Imperium Forged were the empire's deadliest warriors—elite soldiers enhanced with alchemical runes and blood magic. They weren't just trained to kill; they were designed to be unstoppable.

And now they were mobilising.

"Do you think this is about us?" she asked.

Arelan's eyes narrowed. "No."

Althea's stomach twisted. If the empire wasn't sending their war machine after them, who were they going after?

As if in answer, the massive doors of the fortress groaned open. A lone figure emerged, draped in gold and crimson, their face hidden beneath the polished mask of an imperial general. The soldiers in the square snapped to attention as the figure stepped forward, their presence heavy with authority.

Althea's breath caught.

She recognised that mask.

General Cassian Varos.

The Empire's War Machine

The empire's hound. The man who had hunted rogue sorcerers for over a decade.

The man who had nearly caught her once before.

Althea's throat went dry. "We need to leave."

Alan didn't argue.

They slipped out of the cellar, swiftly moving through the winding alleys. The city was a maze of stone and smoke, but Althea knew it well. She had spent too many years hiding in Valcoris's underbelly, slipping through cracks the empire refused to see.

But something felt different tonight.

The streets were too quiet.

The air is too heavy.

Arelan grabbed her wrist suddenly, pulling her into the shadow of an archway. She barely bit back a gasp as a squadron of soldiers passed dangerously close.

They were whispering.

"...deployment orders... heading south..."

"...raiding the villages..."

"... Sorcerer's Rebellion gaining strength..."

Althea's pulse hammered.

The Sorcerer's Rebellion.

She hadn't heard that name in years.

The last remnants of the old world—mages and scholars who had once defied the empire's decree against magic. They had been crushed, burned from history. But if they were rising again if the empire was sending their war machine after them—

It meant war was coming.

Arelan's voice was low. "They're moving to eradicate them before they become a threat."

Althea swallowed hard.

If the rebellion still existed, if there were mages still fighting... then maybe, just maybe, there was hope.

But the empire would never allow it.

She turned to Arelan. "We have to stop them."

Arelan's expression didn't change. "We have to get the artefact."

She scowled. "You heard them. They're going to slaughter people like us. If we don't—"

"They will slaughter us if we waste time."

His voice was sharp, cutting through the night like the edge of a blade.

Althea's chest tightened. "You don't care, do you?"

Arelan's gaze was steady, but something was cold behind his eyes. "Caring doesn't keep people alive."

She clenched her fists. "That's a lie."

Alan exhaled, rubbing a hand over his face. For the first time, he looked… tired.

"If we fail," he said quietly, "none of it will matter."

Althea hated that he was right.

But that didn't mean she had to like it.

They moved quickly, slipping through the crumbling districts of Valcoris until the fortress loomed before them once more. The city's war machine was in motion, but the empire had made one fatal mistake.

They had underestimated them.

Althea turned to Arelan, her voice steady.

"Then let's make sure we don't fail."

Arelan's lips twitched—not quite a smile, but close enough.

They had a war to stop.

And a kingdom to burn.

Six

A Kiss of Power

The fortress walls loomed high, their black stone cold as death under the moonlight. Althea's breath curled in the night air as she pressed her back against the damp stone of a watchtower. Her heart pounded against her ribs, but she forced herself to remain still, invisible in the shadows.

Beside her, Arelan moved without sound, his every step a ghost's whisper. The air was thick with the scent of rain and steel, and below them, the heart of the empire pulsed with quiet menace.

They had made it inside.

But now came the hardest part.

Althea risked a glance down at the courtyard below. Imperial guards moved in controlled patterns, their armor gleaming under the torches that lined the fortress walls. Beyond them, the great doors of the Sanctum of Ash—the emperor's private archive—stood shut. Somewhere inside lay the relic they needed, the key to breaking Arelan's curse.

And possibly something far worse.

Althea exhaled slowly, flexing her fingers. The magic inside her stirred, still sluggish, still weak. She had drained herself too much in the tunnels, and there was no time to recover.

She turned to Arelan. "We need a distraction."

His silver eyes flickered in the dim light. "I'll handle it."

Althea frowned. "That's not a plan, that's a suicide attempt."

Arelan smirked. "I'm very good at surviving."

Before she could protest, he slipped away, his body melding into the darkness like he had been born from it.

Althea cursed under her breath.

Then, below, she heard it.

A sharp whistle—short, precise.

It was a signal.

The guards turned instinctively toward the noise, hands shifting to their swords. In that moment of distraction, Arelan struck.

He moved like a shadow, silent and lethal, cutting through the nearest guard with a flick of his cursed dagger. The blade pulsed as it drank the man's life, and for a moment, the darkness in Arelan's eyes deepened.

Althea's stomach twisted.

It's feeding on him.

She pushed the thought aside and moved.

With the guards thrown into chaos, she darted across the rooftop, her boots barely making a sound. Her target was a narrow window above the archive doors, just small enough for her to squeeze through.

Arelan had done his part. Now it was her turn.

She reached the ledge and swung herself up, gripping the cold stone with trembling fingers. Her muscles screamed in protest, but she ignored them. She had no choice.

The window was locked.

Of course it was.

Althea muttered a curse under her breath and pressed her palm against the glass, focusing what little magic she had left. A flicker of warmth sparked beneath her fingertips, and the lock clicked open.

She slipped inside just as another alarm rang through the courtyard.

She landed softly in the darkened chamber, her heart hammering in her chest. The archive stretched before her, its towering shelves lined with ancient tomes and artifacts stolen from forgotten kingdoms. The air smelled of dust and old magic, thick with the weight of centuries.

She didn't have time to waste.

She moved swiftly, scanning the rows of artifacts for something—anything—that matched the sorcerer's description. A relic of the old gods. A severing stone.

Her fingers traced the bindings of an old book when—

A cold voice echoed through the chamber.

"I wondered when you would show yourself."

Althea whirled.

From the shadows, a man stepped forward, his crimson robes pooling around his feet like spilled blood. His face was hidden behind a golden mask, and when he spoke, his voice was calm, almost amused.

"You've caused quite a bit of trouble tonight."

Althea's pulse spiked. She recognized that voice.

Cassian Varos.

The emperor's right hand. The hunter of sorcerers.

And he was standing between her and the exit.

Althea swallowed hard. "I don't know what you're talking about."

Cassian tilted his head. "Lying doesn't suit you, sorceress."

Althea's grip tightened. She could feel the remnants of her magic stirring, but it wasn't enough. Not against him.

Cassian took a slow step forward. "You seek the Severing Stone."

Althea's breath caught.

He knows.

Cassian chuckled. "You're not the first fool who has tried to steal it."

Althea took a careful step back, her mind racing. "Where is it?"

Cassian hummed, as if considering whether he should answer.

Then, without warning, he lifted a hand.

Pain exploded through Althea's skull.

A force like invisible chains seized her, slamming her back against the nearest bookshelf. She gasped, her vision swimming as books tumbled to the floor around her.

Cassian's magic was different. It wasn't fire, wasn't ice, wasn't shadow. It was pure command.

And it was suffocating.

Althea struggled against the force, but it was like being trapped under a mountain. She could feel it pressing into her ribs, squeezing the air from her lungs.

Cassian watched her impassively.

"Do you know why the Severing Stone is locked away, sorceress?"

Althea clenched her teeth, fighting to keep her vision from blurring.

Cassian stepped closer. "Because it does not break bonds."

His hand curled into a fist, and the pressure around her throat tightened.

"It devours them."

A crackling sound filled the air, a deep, primal hum that sent ice down her spine.

And then—

The doors to the archive exploded inward.

Arelan stood in the wreckage, his dagger gleaming like a dying star. His silver eyes burned with something raw, something dangerous.

Cassian barely had time to react before Arelan moved.

The assassin struck with deadly precision, his blade slicing through the air toward Cassian's throat.

But the golden-masked general was faster.

With a flick of his wrist, Cassian's magic caught the dagger mid-strike, holding it in place like it was suspended in time.

Arelan's jaw tightened.

Cassian sighed. "Predictable."

Then, with a snap of his fingers, he sent Arelan flying back.

The assassin crashed into a marble pillar, his body hitting the stone with a sickening crack.

Althea saw red.

A Spell Between Shadows and Desire

She didn't think. She didn't hesitate.

She let her magic burn.

Fire erupted from her hands, wild and uncontrolled, slamming into Cassian like a wave of molten fury.

For the first time, Cassian's composure faltered.

The golden mask glowed red-hot, the force of the impact sending him staggering back.

The invisible chains around Althea snapped.

She hit the ground hard, gasping for air. Her magic was unraveling, pulling at something deeper inside her, something ancient.

She felt it then—a rush of power that wasn't hers.

A spark of something primal.

She turned, her body moving on instinct.

Arelan was struggling to his feet, his breath ragged. Blood dripped from the corner of his mouth, but his gaze met hers—steady, unwavering.

He was waiting for her signal.

Althea's lips parted.

And then—

Arelan was in front of her.

The room blurred as he pressed his mouth to hers.

The moment their lips met, her magic ignited.

A pulse of raw, unchained power tore through her, through him, and the entire chamber shook.

Cassian staggered back as the force of it sent books and artifacts flying from their shelves.

Arelan's grip on her tightened, his body tense as the power surged between them. It wasn't magic. It was something else.

Something dangerous.

Something alive.

Althea barely had time to process what had happened before Arelan pulled away, his breath shallow, his eyes dark with something she couldn't name.

Cassian cursed under his breath, retreating into the shadows.

Arelan grabbed her wrist.

"Run."

And they did.

Seven

The Assassin's Nightmare

The moment the door slammed shut behind them, the world seemed to fall away. Arelan's chest heaved with every breath, his heart pounding louder than the echo of their footsteps as he dragged Althea through the maze of corridors. His muscles screamed from the strain of both the battle and the magic still thrumming through his veins. But it was the weight in his mind that dragged him down, that gnawed at him like a persistent shadow that refused to fade.

The kiss had been a mistake.

A reckless, unplanned mistake. But worse than that, it had been a reminder—an invitation to something darker, something far worse than the curse that bound him. The power he had felt surging between them, igniting in that moment of urgency, wasn't just magic. It was more. It was dangerous.

He didn't have time to think about it. Not now. Not when they were still running for their lives. But deep down, a part of him knew: this would come for them.

Althea stumbled behind him, her steps quick, her breathing shallow. He could hear the pounding of her pulse as clearly as his own. She had always been strong, always unafraid to face the dangers that came with being what she was. But now, as they moved through the corridors of the Sanctum of Ash, he could feel the weight of her fear. It wasn't from the soldiers that would come searching for them. It was from him. From what he had become.

The relic was within reach. They were so close. He could almost feel it—the pull of it, like a song just beyond his hearing, drawing him in. The Severing Stone was there, hidden deep in the sanctum. But the closer they got to it, the heavier the weight of his curse became.

Arelan's breath hitched as they turned a corner, coming face to face with another set of guards. Their armor gleamed in the torchlight, weapons raised as they stepped into the path.

Althea's hand shot out, her fingers brushing his wrist. Her touch was soft, almost tentative. Her magic had been drained during the battle with Cassian, but she didn't need it. Not yet.

"Do you want to die here?" she whispered, her voice low, sharp with the tension of the moment.

Arelan barely glanced at her, his eyes locked onto the guards.

"If you're asking if I'm going to fight," he said, his voice strained, "then yes."

But Althea had other plans. Before Arelan could even react, she reached for the nearest guard's mind, her magic flaring with what little power remained. The man faltered, his eyes glazing over. The sword in his hand dropped with a soft thud, and the second guard followed suit, his body stiffening as if controlled by invisible strings.

Arelan watched, a faint flicker of surprise in his gaze. "You're getting better."

She didn't smile. "Let's keep moving."

They moved in silence after that, the guards left to their unconscious fates. Althea was always quick to make decisions—bold, fearless in the face of danger. Arelan, however, was more accustomed to moving in the shadows, to waiting for the right moment to strike. But he couldn't afford to wait anymore. Not now. Not with the curse growing heavier, more insistent, twisting his thoughts. The closer they got to the artifact, the harder it was to keep his focus.

He led them deeper into the sanctum, the halls narrowing until they reached a massive iron door. It was marked with an ancient sigil, worn from centuries of neglect. The Severing Stone was on the other side, buried in the vault where the emperor kept his most dangerous treasures.

"Here," Arelan muttered, his fingers brushing the cool metal of the door.

But before he could turn the handle, something—someone—interrupted him.

The air around them chilled. A shadow in the corner of the corridor shifted, and Arelan's hand flew to the hilt of his dagger. He moved, fast, too fast for any normal man, his body in sync with the dark magic that clung to him like a second skin. But before his blade could find its target, the figure stepped forward into the dim light.

It was Cassian.

The general stood there, his golden mask gleaming with an almost ethereal glow. The expression behind it was unreadable, but his stance spoke volumes. He wasn't here to talk.

"You've come for the Stone," Cassian's voice rumbled, deep and calm, as if he had all the time in the world. "I would have thought you knew better, Arelan."

Arelan's breath quickened, but he didn't retreat. "Move," he growled, his voice thick with frustration. He wasn't sure whether it was the battle or the curse that had him on edge, but he knew he couldn't afford to hesitate. Not now. Not when they were so close.

Cassian tilted his head. "I don't think you understand. You aren't the one in control here."

The words hit Arelan like a slap to the face. His grip on the dagger tightened, but he knew what Cassian was implying. The general had always known the truth of Arelan's curse. And it wasn't just a curse anymore—it was a weapon. A trap that he could no longer escape.

"Step aside," Arelan demanded, his voice hoarse.

But Cassian only smiled behind the mask, and the next thing Arelan knew, the general's magic was crashing into him.

It wasn't physical. It wasn't fire or ice. It was the suffocating pressure of control.

Arelan's breath was stolen from his lungs. He couldn't move, couldn't think. It was as if his body had been bound by invisible chains, wrapped so tightly around him that he couldn't even blink. His mind screamed, but his body obeyed. It wasn't his own anymore.

Cassian's magic wrapped around him, pulling at the edges of his soul. "I've seen men like you break," the general said quietly. "I've seen them lose themselves to this curse. And you—" He paused, his voice low. "You're so close, Arelan. So close to losing everything. Your power. Your will. Your soul."

Althea's voice broke through the fog in Arelan's mind. "Arelan!" she shouted, but her voice sounded distant, like she was speaking from far away.

And then, Arelan's mind—his very consciousness—was ripped

open.

He was back in the darkness. The nightmares—the ones that had always haunted him, the ones that lived at the edges of his mind—came rushing in.

He was back on the battlefield, his hands stained with blood. The faces of the men he had killed flashed before him, their lifeless eyes accusing him, cursing him. But it wasn't their voices that haunted him. No. It was the voice of the one who had bound him to the blade. The one who had created him.

"You will kill and you will break. You will be our weapon."

Arelan gasped, struggling against the invisible chains that held him in place.

"The debt is not yet paid, Arelan. You will be ours until the very last drop of your blood is spilled."

The weight of it—of the curse, of the blood magic that bound him—pressed down on him harder, suffocating him. He couldn't breathe. He couldn't think. His vision blurred, and the ground beneath him tilted.

Cassian's voice again, cutting through the darkness like a knife: "This is what you are, Arelan. A broken tool. A weapon to be used and discarded. Just like all the others."

Arelan's breath came in ragged gasps. His eyes snapped open. But he was still bound. He was still trapped.

The Assassin's Nightmare

And Althea—Althea was standing there, helpless.

Arelan forced himself to focus. He couldn't lose himself to the nightmare. Not now. Not when he was so close.

"Althea," he whispered, his voice raw.

Her hand was on his, her warmth cutting through the suffocating darkness. "Arelan," she whispered. "Fight it."

He shook his head, his body trembling with the weight of the magic that threatened to tear him apart. "I can't."

But she didn't let go. Her grip tightened around his wrist, her touch a lifeline in the chaos.

"You're stronger than this," she said, her voice steady. "Don't let him win."

And in that moment—amid the nightmare, amid the chaos—Arelan found something he hadn't felt in years. Hope.

He broke free.

With a guttural scream, Arelan's power surged to the surface. The chains that held him shattered, the darkness that had been closing in on him split apart like shattered glass.

And then, he was himself again.

Cassian staggered back, surprise flashing in his eyes.

"You should have stayed out of this, Arelan," he said, voice tight with frustration.

Arelan didn't answer. His dagger flashed through the air, a silver blur, and for the first time in a long time, he felt his power as it was meant to be. Pure. Unchained.

Cassian fell back, his mask splintering into pieces, his control slipping away.

The nightmare was over. For now.

Eight

The City of Lost Magic

The air was heavy with the scent of rain, as if the city itself were holding its breath. Althea stepped cautiously onto the cracked cobblestones of the forgotten quarter, the weight of the silence pressing down on her. The city of Valcoris was vast, its veins filled with endless corridors of power and politics. But this—this forgotten quarter—was something different. It was a city within a city, a place where time had not only stood still but had actively been erased.

They had found it.

They had found the entrance after hours of searching the alleys and the backstreets. The city of lost magic, hidden beneath layers of dirt and centuries of neglect, where no official maps dared to tread. Its existence had long been thought a myth, a whisper among rogue mages, a story passed down through the ages as a mere legend. But it was real. Althea had always believed it was, and now, as the faint glow of torchlight flickered from the end of a narrow alley, she could feel the power of it—ancient and untamed—filling the air.

Arelan stood beside her, his eyes scanning the path ahead with the same sharp intensity that had gotten them this far. His features were pale under the flickering light, the shadow of exhaustion hanging over him. The remnants of his curse still clung to him, but he wore it with the cold defiance of someone who had learned to fight back, even when the odds were stacked against him.

"Are you sure this is it?" Arelan asked, his voice low, the usual edge of sarcasm absent.

Althea didn't answer immediately. Instead, she closed her eyes, reaching out with the faintest thread of her magic. It responded, sluggishly, as it always did these days, but enough to guide her. She felt the pulse of it, strong and steady, beneath the city's skin.

"This is it," she said finally, her voice barely a whisper. "The lost city… the heart of the old magic."

Arelan's eyes flicked toward her, a frown tugging at his lips. He didn't trust the idea of magic this old—this uncontrolled. Althea didn't blame him. The curse that had bound him for so long had soured his view of magic. It wasn't something that could be controlled or wielded without consequence. It was dangerous. It was alive.

But this was different. This was their only chance.

They continued, their footsteps echoing as they moved deeper into the alley, toward the ruins that lay ahead. The buildings around them were half-collapsed, their stone walls eaten away by time and neglect. The windows were shattered, the doorways gaping, as though the city itself had given up trying to hold on to the past. Yet even in this decay, there was something beautiful—something haunting about it. Magic had once flowed here. It had once thrived. And now, it was a memory, long lost, waiting for someone to find it again.

Althea could feel it in her bones. The power was still there, lurking just beneath the surface, waiting to be awakened. She could taste it in the air, sharp and unfamiliar, like the crackle before a storm.

They reached the heart of the quarter, where the ruins gave way to a large courtyard. The center of the courtyard was dominated by a vast fountain, dry and cracked, but its once-grand stonework still stood tall, like an ancient sentinel guarding the secrets of the past. The stones around it were covered in thick vines and creeping moss, and there, in the center, lay a stone slab—the entrance to the underground city that had been forgotten for so long.

Althea could hear the hum now, louder and clearer, as if it were calling to her.

"This is it," she said, her voice barely above a whisper. She knelt before the stone slab, brushing her fingers over the weathered surface. There were no markings, no sigils, nothing to indicate that this was anything more than a forgotten relic. But she knew. She had always known.

Arelan crouched beside her, his gaze lingering on the slab. He didn't need to ask. He trusted her. They had been through enough together by now. The tension between them was still there, simmering just beneath the surface, but it was different now. There was a connection—a shared understanding of what was at stake.

"Can you feel it?" Althea asked softly, her fingers still brushing the cold stone. "It's alive. This place—this city—was built on magic. The kind of magic that's older than the empire, older than the kingdoms. It's not just power, Arelan. It's… something else."

He didn't respond immediately. Instead, his eyes narrowed as he looked around them, his hand hovering near his dagger. He wasn't so quick to trust magic these days. Neither of them were. But there was something about the weight of the air around them—something that felt like the edge of a precipice.

"You don't trust it, do you?" Althea said, glancing up at him.

He didn't look away. "I don't trust anything anymore."

Althea's lips pressed into a tight line. She knew exactly what he meant. The curse, the blade, the empire—it had all shattered

The City of Lost Magic

any belief in simple truths. Nothing was ever what it seemed.

But she had to believe in this. They had to believe in this.

Taking a deep breath, she closed her eyes and focused. Her magic—weak though it was—began to pulse in rhythm with the hum of the ancient city, a gentle vibration that seemed to come from the very heart of the stone beneath her hands. The power here was unlike anything she had felt before. It was raw. It was untamed. It was the old magic.

Her fingers traced the edge of the slab, and the moment she touched a specific mark hidden beneath the moss and vines, a sharp, sudden click reverberated through the ground beneath them.

The stone began to shift.

Arelan cursed under his breath as the ground trembled, but Althea didn't flinch. She had been expecting this. The magic had chosen her. She could feel it, sinking into her like a second skin, wrapping around her soul and pulling her forward. This place had been waiting for someone to unlock it, and now that someone was her.

The stone slab slid aside, revealing a narrow staircase that descended into the darkness below. The air that wafted up from the passage was cool, heavy with the scent of dust and old secrets.

"We're not the first to come looking for this," Arelan murmured, his voice low and wary. "I don't like this, Althea. There's something wrong here."

She turned to face him, her eyes flashing with determination. "We don't have a choice, Arelan. This is our only chance."

Without waiting for his reply, she stepped into the darkness, her senses tingling as the magic surged around her.

The stairs seemed endless, winding down into the depths of the earth. The walls of the passage were rough-hewn, the stone jagged and uneven, as if it had been carved by hands long gone. The air grew colder the deeper they descended, the sound of their footsteps echoing off the walls like a warning.

Althea's magic responded to the darkness, pulsing faintly in her veins, but it wasn't enough. She needed more. She needed the power that had been locked away in this city. She needed the Severing Stone.

They reached the bottom, where the passage opened into a vast underground chamber. The ceiling was lost in shadow, but Althea could feel the weight of it—the enormity of what lay hidden in the heart of the city.

In the center of the room stood a pedestal, and atop it, glowing faintly in the dim light, was the Severing Stone. It was a jagged crystal, dark and fractured, yet pulsing with an energy that could not be ignored.

Althea felt it before she saw it—the unmistakable pull, like a magnetic force drawing her toward it. It was the heart of this place, the source of the magic that had been buried for so long.

She stepped forward, but as she did, something shifted in the shadows.

A figure stepped from the darkness.

A figure she had never thought to see again.

The man was tall, his face masked by a hood that obscured everything except the faint glow of his eyes. He moved with the quiet grace of a predator, his presence so strong that it seemed to fill the entire room.

Arelan's voice was a low growl behind her. "No. Not him."

But Althea couldn't tear her gaze away. She had seen him once before.

The sorcerer.

The one who had bound Arelan to the blade. The one who had been pulling the strings from the shadows.

He stepped forward, his voice low and cold. "You've found it, then. The heart of the old magic."

Althea's blood ran cold.

But she didn't back down. "What do you want?"

A Spell Between Shadows and Desire

The sorcerer's smile was a twisted thing, full of dark amusement. "What do I want? I want what's mine."

He raised a hand, and the ground beneath them trembled.

The Severing Stone glowed brighter. And with it, the world seemed to shift.

Althea's heart skipped a beat.

Nine

Dancing on the Edge of Desire

The room seemed to pulse with a life of its own, the shadows flickering and shifting like living things. Althea stood frozen, her gaze locked on the sorcerer as he moved closer, each step deliberate, his presence so overpowering that it felt like the very air around them had thickened.

Arelan's hand was a constant weight at her side, his fingers twitching toward his dagger, but his posture was tense, ready to spring into action at the first sign of trouble. The sorcerer hadn't drawn any weapon, but he didn't need to. His magic was his weapon—powerful, ancient, and beyond anything they had faced so far.

Althea could feel it, the way his presence in the room seemed to reach into her bones and twist her insides. The Severing

Stone pulsed with an unnatural energy, its jagged edges glowing brighter with each passing second. The power it radiated was intoxicating, but it was also dangerous. Althea knew that.

"Why?" she asked, her voice hoarse, barely above a whisper. "Why are you here?"

The sorcerer stopped just a few paces away from her, and though his face was hidden beneath the shadow of his hood, Althea could sense the smile in his voice. It was a slow, almost predatory smile.

"You know why," he replied, his tone dripping with dark amusement. "The Stone has always been mine to control. It is the source of everything, the key to more power than you can possibly comprehend."

Althea's eyes narrowed. "You're not getting it."

She could feel the curse inside Arelan, the dark magic that still clung to him, but it wasn't just the curse that unsettled her. It was the pull of the Severing Stone—the same pull that had drawn her in from the very moment she'd stepped into the forgotten city. The Stone was calling to her, whispering promises of power, of liberation, of breaking every chain that had ever bound her. But it wasn't her freedom it sought. It was hers to control, to consume, to possess.

The sorcerer tilted his head, as if amused by her defiance. "You're a fool to resist," he said softly. "This power could be yours. All you need to do is reach out and claim it."

The words stirred something inside her, a fire that had been burning just below the surface, something that wanted to rise, something that craved release. For a moment, Althea's mind wavered, the vision of untold power flashing before her eyes. But then she looked at Arelan, standing beside her, his presence a steady anchor in the sea of temptation.

It was him. It was always him.

Her breath hitched as their eyes met, the connection between them crackling like electricity. There was something in his gaze, something that spoke of shared pain, shared battles, and—strangely—shared longing.

The sorcerer chuckled, sensing the tension between them. "Ah, yes. The bond between you two. It's undeniable, isn't it?"

Althea felt the blood drain from her face. The sorcerer's voice, though still laced with amusement, held an edge of something darker. "Don't think for a second that I don't see what's between you."

Arelan's fingers twitched at his dagger, but he didn't draw it. Althea could feel the quiet battle inside him, the same pull of temptation that she had felt, urging him to act, to strike, to end this. But he didn't. He wouldn't. Not yet.

The sorcerer's voice softened, his next words a quiet whisper, as though he were speaking directly into her mind. "Do you think you're the first to feel the weight of this Stone? Do you think you're the first to come close to it and then pull away?

I have seen many like you, Althea. Many who thought they could walk away from the power it offers. But it never lets go."

His words seemed to worm their way into her thoughts, sinking in like poison. The temptation of the Stone was too great, too seductive to resist. For a moment, she felt herself drawn to it, the magnetic pull of it like an invisible thread around her soul.

Her hand reached out, but before she could touch the Stone, Arelan grabbed her wrist, his grip tight enough to hurt. His voice was low, barely a whisper, but it was steady, grounded.

"Don't."

For a moment, she wanted to pull away, to tear herself free, to claim what was rightfully hers. But Arelan's touch held her steady, grounding her in reality. He was her anchor.

She didn't pull away.

Instead, she turned her gaze to him, meeting his eyes. There was something unspoken between them, something they had both ignored for so long, buried beneath the weight of their mission, their curses, their history. But now, in this moment, with the very essence of magic thrumming in the air, that bond felt undeniable.

And yet—

Arelan's grip on her wrist tightened. His breath was ragged, but he said nothing. He didn't need to. Althea knew what he was feeling. She could feel it too. The ache between them. The pull. The desire.

It was too much.

The sorcerer laughed, his voice rich with dark amusement. "Isn't it beautiful?" he asked, gesturing to the Stone. "The way it calls to you both, how it knows what you crave."

Althea's breath caught in her throat. The pull was stronger now, more insistent, like a siren's call. She could feel it in the air, in her bones, in the very core of her being. And the part of her that had always been hungry for power, for freedom, for release, surged to the surface.

Arelan's fingers tightened, almost painfully, around her wrist, but there was something else in his eyes now, something fierce. He wasn't holding her back just to stop her from touching the Stone. He was holding her back because he was afraid of what would happen if they both gave in to that temptation.

"Althea," he whispered, his voice ragged, barely controlled. "We can't. Not like this."

The desire—no, the need—to let go, to give in to the Stone's power, surged through her like wildfire. But she didn't act on it. Not yet.

The sorcerer took a step forward, his eyes glinting with dark amusement. "You think you can control it, Arelan? You think you can keep her from it? From what she really wants?"

A Spell Between Shadows and Desire

Althea felt the burn in her chest, the weight of his words sinking in. She had always been drawn to the darkness, to the forbidden magic that had called to her since the moment she had first touched it. She had always wanted more—more than the world had ever given her. But now, with Arelan at her side, she felt torn.

The Stone called to her. The curse called to Arelan. But it was them, together, that made everything feel so uncertain, so dangerous.

The sorcerer's eyes gleamed, reading her like an open book. "You're both playing a dangerous game," he said. "But it's a game you'll never win. Not unless you embrace the truth of what you are. What you could be."

Arelan stepped forward, his eyes flashing. "We're not what you say we are. We're not your pawns."

The sorcerer's smile widened. "Oh, but you are. And I'll enjoy watching you both burn."

Before Althea could react, before she could move, the sorcerer raised his hand. The air shimmered, and the Stone flared with a brilliant light, blinding her for a moment.

Then, just as suddenly, everything stopped. The Stone's light dimmed, and the air grew still.

Arelan's hand tightened around her wrist again, pulling her to him, his body pressed against hers. His breath was harsh, his chest rising and falling as if he, too, had felt the suffocating weight of that power.

And in that moment, their gazes locked, and something passed between them—something more than desire, more than need. It was a recognition of truth.

They were teetering on the edge of something far greater than either of them could control.

And neither of them was ready to fall.

Ten

Betrayal Under Moonlight

The moon hung high in the sky, its pale light casting long shadows across the ruins of the ancient city. The courtyard was empty, save for the faint echo of Althea's and Arelan's footsteps. The air was thick with tension, the promise of something yet to come. They had narrowly escaped the sorcerer's trap, the power of the Severing Stone still simmering beneath their skin, but the weight of what they had just endured hung heavy between them.

Arelan's hand brushed against his side where his dagger usually rested, but tonight, it felt heavier. He could feel the curse stirring within him again, the dark magic pulsing at the edges of his mind, tempting him to embrace it. It was always there, always waiting, but it was stronger now. It felt like the very ground beneath his feet was shifting, like the world was trying to pull him into the abyss.

Althea walked beside him, her steps as silent as his own, but there was a distance in her gaze that he hadn't seen before. It wasn't just the fear of what they had faced in the underground city—it was something deeper, something more unsettling. The temptation to reach for the Stone, to claim its power, had affected them both. But for Althea, it had been different. She had wanted it. And the way she had looked at him—her hesitation, her need—had shaken him.

The silence between them was suffocating, but neither of them broke it as they moved through the city. The further they walked, the more Arelan felt the pull of the curse, like invisible chains pulling him back toward the ruins. But there was something else—something more urgent. There were eyes on them.

He wasn't sure how long they had been walking before they reached the edge of the courtyard. The shadows grew deeper, longer, as if the night itself had wrapped around them like a blanket. The distant sound of the city felt muffled, like the world had fallen away, leaving only the two of them in this suspended moment. But that was when it happened. The whisper of movement, the flicker of something—or someone— just out of reach.

Althea's breath hitched beside him. She had sensed it too.

"Stay close," Arelan muttered, his hand instinctively reaching for his dagger, though he knew it wouldn't be enough. The curse, the power of the Severing Stone—it had made him reckless. Made him more dangerous. He couldn't trust himself.

But he could trust her. Or so he thought.

They turned a corner, and the figure emerged from the darkness, stepping into the dim light with the casual grace of someone who had always belonged there.

Arelan froze. His heart skipped a beat.

It was Cassian.

The general's golden mask gleamed in the moonlight, his figure framed by the ruins of the city. There was no hint of surprise on his face, only the quiet confidence of someone who had already won. His posture was relaxed, but his eyes—those cold, calculating eyes—were fixed on Althea.

"Did you really think you could escape?" Cassian's voice was smooth, like silk, but laced with an edge that made the hairs on the back of Arelan's neck stand on end.

Althea's hand twitched, her fingers grazing her side where her own weapon was sheathed, but she didn't draw it. She stood still, facing the general, but Arelan could see the flicker of uncertainty in her eyes. The same uncertainty that had been creeping into her gaze ever since the sorcerer's last words.

"You…" Arelan's voice was tight, the rage building in his chest, but he couldn't speak. He couldn't breathe. Cassian was here—standing between them and freedom.

"You thought you could walk away from the Stone," Cassian

continued, taking a step closer. "From its pull. From everything you've ever known. But there's no escaping it, not now. Not with the power you've unleashed."

Althea didn't respond. She didn't move. But Arelan could feel the tension in her, the way she was fighting against something deep inside her, something that threatened to rise again. The same thing that had drawn her toward the Stone in the first place. It was too much.

And then, just as quickly as the anger had flared, a sudden thought flickered in Arelan's mind. Something wasn't right. Something was wrong. Cassian's voice, the way he had spoken. The look in his eyes.

He turned to Althea, ready to warn her, ready to tell her to stay back. But when his eyes met hers, the world seemed to shift.

Althea stepped forward.

And she did something Arelan hadn't expected.

She lowered her weapon.

"Cassian," she said softly, her voice almost tender, though the air around them crackled with tension. Arelan's heart skipped a beat. What was happening?

"Althea," Cassian said in return, his voice like a caress. There was no hostility, no anger. Just a calm that was almost too serene. "You and I both know that this has always been inevitable."

Arelan's stomach dropped. This wasn't just about the Stone. It wasn't about the curse. It was something more. Something deeper.

"No," Arelan rasped. He stepped toward Althea, his hand reaching for her arm, pulling her back, but she didn't resist. Her gaze didn't even waver from Cassian.

"Althea," he said again, his voice low, more urgent this time. "What is this? What's going on?"

But Althea didn't answer. Instead, she tilted her head, her lips curling into something that wasn't quite a smile.

"It was always going to happen this way, Arelan," she said, her voice soft, almost apologetic.

Arelan's grip on her arm tightened. "No. This isn't you. This is—" He stopped, his voice faltering as something cold ran through him. He looked at Cassian, then back at her. "What are you saying?"

Cassian took another step forward, his gaze flickering between them. "The Stone calls to her. You know that, don't you, Arelan? She's been resisting it—fighting it. But now…" He smiled, the look in his eyes growing more dangerous. "Now she sees it. She understands."

The truth settled over Arelan like a heavy fog. His breath

hitched, his body trembling with the weight of it. He could feel the heat in Althea's eyes now, the way she was looking at him—not with affection, not with the warmth they had shared, but with something cold. Something distant.

And that was when he understood.

She was never meant to fight the curse.

She was meant to embrace it.

Althea's fingers twitched, and the air between them shimmered, crackling with dark magic. Arelan recoiled as the magic that had been dormant inside her surged, filling the space around them with a power so intense it nearly knocked him off his feet.

"You…" His voice faltered as he took a step back, his heart sinking. "You betrayed me."

The words cut through the silence like a blade.

Althea didn't answer. She didn't need to. The truth was in her eyes. It was in the way her magic pulsed around her, the way her lips parted in something that could have been a smile—or a smirk.

Arelan stood there, stunned, his chest tight with disbelief. "All this time," he whispered, his voice breaking. "You've been using me."

She didn't flinch.

Cassian stepped forward, his gaze never leaving Arelan. "You were never part of her plan. Not really. She only needed you to get to the Stone. To unlock the door."

Arelan's mind raced, the pieces of the puzzle falling into place too late. The way she had looked at him before, her hesitation—that wasn't fear. It had been something else. Something darker.

The Stone had never been her goal. She had used him to get to it. And now, it was hers.

He felt sick. He felt betrayed.

And in that moment, he realized something that shook him to his core—Althea wasn't the woman he thought she was.

"Goodbye, Arelan," Althea said softly, her voice laced with something like regret—but only for herself. She was already turning away, stepping toward Cassian.

The moonlight above them cast long, thin shadows, and as she moved toward the general, the betrayal in her eyes was clear. She had made her choice.

But so had he.

Arelan drew his dagger. The weight of it was nothing compared to the weight in his chest, the cold realization that the one person he had trusted, the one person he had thought could be his salvation, had betrayed him.

But no more.

With a flash of silver, he lunged.

Eleven

A Curse That Binds Two Souls

The darkness seemed to stretch infinitely in every direction, swallowing everything in its wake. Arelan's heart beat a frantic rhythm, the pulse of betrayal echoing in his chest. His breath came in sharp gasps, but he didn't stop. He couldn't. Not now. Not when the truth of Althea's betrayal burned through him like wildfire.

His dagger was still in his hand, slick with the sweat of his own palms, the cold steel a heavy weight. But no matter how tightly he gripped it, no matter how hard he tried to focus on what needed to be done, the image of Althea's eyes—the coldness in them as she walked away from him—kept replaying in his mind.

The moment she turned her back on him, he felt it. The curse, the darkness that had always been just below the surface, began to twist and writhe, urging him to embrace the power of the Severing Stone.

A voice echoed in his mind. It was familiar, twisted with time, like a fading memory.

"You are bound, Arelan. The debt is not yet paid."

The voice of the one who had cursed him, who had made him into a weapon—someone who had never had a choice. But now, with Althea's betrayal settling deep into his soul, something inside him began to break.

Alone.

He was alone.

And that was when the curse came alive.

The familiar magic that had once felt like a weight now surged within him like a wave of raw power, overwhelming him, consuming him from the inside out. Arelan's body trembled as the shadows around him began to twist and bend, the air growing thick with dark energy. He could feel the power inside him, far more potent than it had ever been, but it was no longer something he could control. It was him.

His vision blurred as his grip tightened on his dagger, the silver blade catching the moonlight that filtered through the ruins. His teeth ground together as the curse swelled inside him, threatening to break free. The magic, ancient and dark, was calling to him, urging him to use it—to let it consume him, to let it claim him. He could feel it, like a thousand voices whispering in his mind, a choir of forgotten souls crying out for release.

And then, as if summoned by his darkest thoughts, the shadows around him grew still.

He was no longer alone.

A shape materialized from the darkness, moving with the fluid grace of a predator in the night.

Arelan's heart skipped a beat, and he instinctively raised his dagger. His breath was ragged, the power of the curse swelling within him, threatening to break free. But the figure in front of him didn't make a move. It didn't need to.

It was her.

Althea.

She stood before him, her figure bathed in the faint glow of the moonlight, her eyes dark and unreadable. The way she looked at him now was different—colder, more distant, as if the distance between them had grown beyond anything they had ever shared.

He opened his mouth to speak, but no words came.

The connection between them had always been undeniable, but now, it was a fracture. Something had changed.

Her voice broke the silence, soft and unyielding.

"I'm sorry, Arelan."

He flinched, as if the words themselves had struck him.

"Sorry?" he repeated, his voice hoarse, cracked with disbelief. "Sorry for what? For using me? For leading me into this? For betraying me?"

Althea's eyes flickered, a shadow passing over them. "I never wanted it to be this way," she said, her voice barely above a whisper, like the breath of a storm. "But the power of the Severing Stone…it changes everything. You and I—we were always meant to find it. To be part of it."

Arelan's hands clenched, his dagger slipping through his fingers as his chest tightened. The anger that had been boiling inside him—the frustration, the betrayal—began to burn. He stepped toward her, the words spilling from his mouth before he could stop them.

"We were never meant to be part of it, Althea. We were never meant to be part of your game."

She didn't retreat, didn't flinch. She stood there, calm and unwavering, a cold mask of regret on her face.

"The curse that binds us, Arelan," she began, her voice steady, "it's not just something that you carry. It's something we both carry." She met his gaze, and for the first time, he saw the truth in her eyes—the same dark truth that had been burning between them all along. "It's always been us. This... this destiny."

"Destiny?" he spat, the word bitter on his tongue. "You call this destiny? You used me to unlock the Stone. You used me to break the curse. And now—now you're telling me this is our destiny?"

Her silence was deafening, but the flicker of something—regret—moved through her gaze.

Arelan took a step back, his thoughts a tangle of confusion and betrayal. His chest felt hollow, empty. The curse twisted within him, feeding off the emotions, the pain. The more he fought it, the stronger it became. But something was different now. He could feel it. It was alive. It wasn't just bound to him anymore. It was feeding off their pain, their anger.

It was feeding off the bond between them.

The power surged again, and this time, Arelan couldn't stop it. His magic—the curse—began to take control, bending his will as if it were nothing more than a toy. The shadows around them seemed to reach for him, pulling him into the darkness. The air thickened, crackling with energy.

"Don't do this, Arelan," Althea's voice rang out, softer now, almost pleading. "You're not thinking clearly."

He looked at her, his eyes burning with frustration and the

swirling rage that was coursing through him. "What do you want me to think, Althea?" he growled. "That you've done nothing wrong? That I'm still the same fool who followed you?"

The shadows around them began to writhe, closing in, dark tendrils curling around his body, pulling at his soul. He felt the weight of them, the curse tightening its grip on him as though it had always been there, waiting.

And then, something broke.

The stone beneath their feet trembled, and with a burst of light, the Severing Stone pulsed. It was a violent, radiant shockwave, sending both of them staggering back. The force of it knocked them off balance, but the pull of the Stone was undeniable. Althea's hands trembled as she reached out toward it, her face a mix of longing and hesitation. The power was too great, and Arelan knew she wouldn't be able to resist much longer.

"You can't control it," Arelan warned, his voice strained. The curse within him was tightening, suffocating him, but his focus never wavered. Not now. "The Stone—this power—it's not yours to take."

Her eyes flickered to the Stone, and then back to him. The bond between them, the connection, was still there. She could feel it too. The same magnetism. The same force that had brought them together, that had pulled them into this place.

"You think you're the only one who's trapped in this, Arelan?" Her voice broke, and there was something in it—desperation—that made his heart clench. "You think I wanted this? I didn't. But I don't have a choice anymore." She stepped closer to the Stone. "I can't keep running from it. From this—us."

Arelan's chest tightened, his heart racing as the shadows continued to grow, pushing at the edges of his mind. The power was consuming him. But in that moment, there was something else—something deeper. The curse wasn't just binding him to the Stone. It was binding him to her.

"Don't," he whispered, reaching out to her, his voice thick with emotion. "Don't let it consume you."

Althea's fingers brushed the Stone, and with that simple touch, everything seemed to stop. The darkness swirled around them, the very air charged with power. But there was a moment—just a single, fleeting moment—where the curse inside them both seemed to quiet.

And then it happened.

The Stone reacted. It was a sudden, blinding flash, and Arelan's body locked up, as if the magic had seized him entirely. Althea gasped, her hand still hovering near the Stone as if she could stop it from releasing its full force. But it was too late. The Stone had claimed them both.

A scream ripped through the silence, but it wasn't just Althea's. It was Arelan's too. A sharp, unbearable pain that cut through him like nothing he'd ever felt before. The curse surged in his veins, twisting, breaking apart everything in its wake.

And in that instant, he realized: the Stone didn't just bind them. It merged them.

Two souls. One curse.

Althea's breath hitched as she staggered back, feeling the weight of the magic binding them tighter than ever before. She couldn't move, couldn't breathe, as the full force of the Stone's power crashed into her chest. And in that moment, she realized she wasn't just bound to the Stone—she was bound to him.

They were one.

Twelve

The Emperor's Deception

The air in the Emperor's throne room was thick with tension, heavy with the scent of old incense and polished stone. Arelan's footsteps echoed sharply against the cold marble floor as he entered, his boots clicking with a deliberate rhythm. The massive doors behind him creaked shut with an almost finality, sealing him into the room with the one man who had orchestrated everything.

The throne room stretched high, its vaulted ceilings lost in shadows, the walls adorned with gold and crimson banners—the colors of the empire. But it wasn't the opulence that caught Arelan's eye. It was the man seated on the throne, his back straight and regal, his eyes hidden beneath the veil of his golden mask. The Emperor.

There was an unsettling stillness in the air, like the calm before a storm. The Emperor's presence was suffocating, as though the very weight of his power radiated from him, filling the space with an oppressive force. Arelan's stomach twisted as he stood there, waiting, the weight of what he had just learned bearing down on him like an anchor. His mind was racing, trying to piece together the fragments of truth he had uncovered, but it felt like he was standing on the edge of a precipice, unsure of how far he was willing to fall.

"So," the Emperor's voice cut through the silence, smooth and practiced, "you've come."

Arelan didn't answer immediately. He couldn't. His hands clenched into fists, the raw anger he had felt ever since discovering the truth bubbling to the surface. The truth about the Emperor, about the curse, and about Althea. The betrayal ran deeper than he had ever imagined.

"I thought you might have learned by now," the Emperor continued, his voice laced with condescension. "That I always get what I want."

Arelan's pulse quickened. He took a step forward, each movement slow, calculated. "You knew, didn't you?" His voice was strained, but steady. "From the beginning. From the moment you cursed me. This wasn't about me being your weapon. This was about using her." He spat the words, his gaze never leaving the Emperor.

The Emperor didn't move. He didn't need to. His mask gleamed in the dim light, an impassive expression that betrayed nothing. "Her?" The Emperor's tone was amused, as though Arelan had said something trivial. "You always were blind, Arelan. To the truth. To your purpose. To her purpose."

The words hit Arelan like a slap. Her purpose. That was it, wasn't it? Althea had never been part of his plan. She was never meant to stand with him, to fight alongside him. She was always meant to be a tool—a key to unlocking the deeper, darker magic. Arelan's chest tightened as the truth slammed into him with a force he wasn't ready for. She had used him. She had always used him.

"You used her," Arelan growled, the anger in his voice rising. "And you used me. To break the curse. To claim the Stone. And now…" His voice faltered as the weight of it hit him. "Now you have what you wanted."

The Emperor's eyes narrowed, but his voice remained calm, almost patient. "You still don't understand, do you? You were always a pawn, Arelan. But even pawns have their purpose. Your role in this was never as important as hers."

Arelan's stomach lurched. Hers. The Emperor had always known. He had known about the bond between them. He had known how Althea would react, how she would be drawn to the Stone, how she would let herself fall into the temptation of its power.

"And now that you've served your purpose," the Emperor said, his words like daggers, "it's time to see just how much you're willing to sacrifice for your freedom."

The Emperor's Deception

The words cut through Arelan, chilling him to his very core. Freedom? He had thought he was fighting for freedom. But he had never been free. None of them had been.

Before Arelan could respond, the Emperor rose from his throne, his movements graceful, almost predatory. The silence in the room deepened as he descended the steps, his golden mask glinting with every step.

"Do you understand now, Arelan?" The Emperor's voice was like silk, but there was an edge to it. "You've always been a means to an end. But she..." He paused, his eyes flickering toward the door. "She was always the key."

Arelan's eyes followed the Emperor's gaze, and for a moment, time seemed to slow. The door to the throne room creaked open, and a figure stepped inside.

It was Althea.

Her eyes were fixed on the Emperor, and her presence was like a storm cloud hanging over the room. The same woman who had stood beside him, fought beside him. The same woman who had, in a single moment, shattered everything he had believed.

Arelan's heart pounded in his chest as she walked toward him, her steps slow, deliberate. Her eyes—those same eyes—met his, but there was no recognition in them. No warmth. Only coldness.

"You..." Arelan's voice cracked. He tried to move toward her, but his legs felt like they were made of stone, frozen in place. The betrayal—her betrayal—was still too raw.

She didn't speak at first. She merely stopped a few feet away from him, standing tall, her hands clenched at her sides. Her expression was unreadable, but Arelan could see the tension in her body, the way her shoulders were drawn tight, as though she were holding something back.

"Arelan," she finally said, her voice calm, but there was something in the way she said his name that made his blood run cold. "I didn't want this." Her eyes flickered to the Emperor before returning to him, but there was no apology in her gaze. There was only resolve.

"Didn't want this?" Arelan's laugh was bitter, edged with disbelief. "You've been playing me, Althea. From the start. Using me. Using us." His voice shook with the weight of the words, the anger rising again. "You lied to me."

"I didn't lie," she replied softly. "I never lied."

Her words hung in the air like a taunt, and Arelan could feel his chest tightening with each breath. The curse inside him was stirring again, louder, stronger, feeding off the emotions crashing inside him. He fought it, but the more he fought, the more it wanted to consume him. The Emperor's words echoed in his mind, urging him to embrace it, to let the power of the curse break him, to break her.

But it was her—it had always been her—that had made him

feel something more than the curse. The bond between them was undeniable, and yet it felt like the very thing that was now tearing him apart.

"I never wanted to hurt you," Althea said, her voice barely above a whisper, but there was no trace of guilt in her expression. Only cold resolution. "But I had no choice."

"No choice?" Arelan's voice rose. "You used me. You used us both."

"I did what I had to do," Althea replied, her voice steady, her eyes never leaving his. "To break the chains. To stop the empire. To stop the curse."

Arelan stepped back, his hands shaking with the force of his own emotions. The air around him felt heavy, charged with the power of the curse, with the magic that surged beneath the surface. But it wasn't just the curse that had him trapped. It was the way Althea was looking at him now—like she had already decided the outcome. Like she had already made her choice.

The Emperor chuckled, a soft, menacing sound that echoed through the room. "You see, Arelan," he said, his voice low and thick with amusement, "you were never part of the plan. Not truly. Althea and I—we've been working toward this moment for a long time. You were just a tool. A means to an end."

Arelan's eyes snapped to Althea, his heart breaking with the realization that he had been nothing more than a pawn in her game. The bond between them, the moments they had shared, the battles they had fought side by side—it had all been a lie.

A cruel, cruel lie.

And in that moment, with the Emperor standing behind her, Althea didn't look like the woman he had once trusted. She looked like a stranger.

"No," Arelan said, his voice barely a whisper. "No…" He shook his head, as though the words could somehow undo the truth. But the truth was there.

And it was crushing him.

Althea took a step forward, her eyes softening for just a moment before the mask of coldness returned. "I'm sorry," she said again, her voice breaking, but it didn't reach him. Not anymore.

The Emperor's laughter filled the silence. "You'll understand soon enough, Arelan. The curse binds you both. The magic binds you both. There's no escaping it now."

Arelan didn't speak. He didn't move. He was frozen in place, his heart a cold, empty void as the realization sank in. This was the Emperor's deception. This was what he had planned all along. The curse. The Stone. Althea.

And now, there was no way out.

Thirteen

A Kingdom of Shadows

The cold wind swept through the vast hallways of the Imperial Palace, the high stone walls seeming to absorb every sound, every movement, until the silence was almost suffocating. Arelan could feel it closing in around him, the weight of it pressing against his chest, as though the very air in the palace was thick with the tension of what had come to pass. He hadn't moved for what felt like an eternity, his eyes fixed on the Emperor, whose golden mask gleamed coldly in the low light.

Beside him, Althea stood still, her gaze averted, her shoulders tense. The woman he had trusted, the woman he had fought beside, now seemed like a ghost, a stranger wrapped in the same flesh that once held his heart. She hadn't spoken since the Emperor's cruel revelation—the truth of their bond, their fate, and the role she had played in shaping it.

The realization had cut through Arelan like a blade. The curse had never been his to fight alone. It had always been a shared burden, a shared trap, set by the Emperor to control them both. The Severing Stone, the magic binding them together— it was all part of a larger plan, a scheme he couldn't yet fully understand.

As he stood there, the weight of betrayal still fresh in his chest, Arelan felt his thoughts spiral. The Emperor, the man who had orchestrated all of this, stood at the center of it all, a puppet master pulling the strings, laughing at them, controlling them. But what was his true purpose? What did he want with Althea?

"You still don't understand, do you?" The Emperor's voice broke the stillness, the smoothness of it almost too much to bear. "You think you're free. That you've chosen your path. But you haven't. You never will."

The Emperor took a step forward, his every movement deliberate, as though he was savoring the moment. "The curse binds you, Arelan. Not just to the Stone. Not just to your fate. But to her." He looked at Althea, his eyes cold beneath the mask. "And in time, you'll both see the truth. You were never meant to be free."

Althea flinched at the words, but didn't respond. She had been quiet for so long that Arelan wasn't sure she would ever speak again. She had never wanted this. He could see that now. But how could he ever know for certain what had truly driven her? Was it the promise of power? Was it her own desire for freedom, the same as his? Or was she simply another pawn in the Emperor's endless game?

Arelan turned toward her, searching her face for any sign of recognition, for any shred of the woman he had known. "Althea…" His voice was low, broken. "What is this? Tell me the truth."

She didn't answer. She couldn't. The distance between them felt insurmountable, a chasm that had opened up between them, and no matter how hard he tried, he couldn't reach her.

The Emperor chuckled softly, his voice smooth like velvet. "It's simple, really," he said, his eyes gleaming beneath the mask. "The Stone is a tool. A vessel of power, yes. But more importantly, it is a bridge. A bridge that links you both—your magic, your souls. When you embraced it, when you allowed it to connect you, you became part of something greater. Something ancient."

Arelan's stomach churned. He had suspected as much. The Stone, the magic—it had always been more than just a curse. It had always been a connection, a bond between him and Althea. But the implications were terrifying. He could feel it now, in the way his magic swirled beneath his skin, in the way her presence seemed to reach him even when she was far away. They were connected. But what did that mean for them?

"You see," the Emperor continued, his voice growing darker, "you've both been caught in the web of a kingdom of shadows, a place where the light never reaches. You've never truly been free. The empire is built on the backs of those who serve it.

And you, Arelan," he said, turning his attention back to him, "you've served it from the very beginning. You just didn't know it."

The words struck Arelan like a physical blow. He staggered back, the weight of them pushing him down, trying to crush him. The Emperor's laughter echoed in his ears, taunting, mocking. It was all coming together now—his curse, his role in this twisted game, the way Althea had always been a part of it.

"Enough," Arelan growled, taking a step toward the Emperor, his hands shaking with rage. "I've had enough of your games. Enough of your lies."

But before he could take another step, Althea moved.

It was swift—quicker than Arelan could react. She stepped between him and the Emperor, her body blocking his path, and her eyes met his with an intensity that sent a chill through him. The soft flicker of light from the torches cast shadows across her face, but the coldness in her gaze was undeniable.

"You can't stop him, Arelan," she said, her voice a whisper, but it was filled with finality. "You don't understand. None of us do. This is bigger than us. Bigger than you."

Arelan's chest tightened. His heart raced. He had heard the Emperor's words, but he refused to believe them. "No. This isn't bigger than us. We can stop him. We can stop this."

Althea shook her head slowly, her fingers twitching, as if she were fighting to hold something back. She stepped closer to him, her face inches from his, and he could feel the cold distance between them, the way the bond that had once held them together now seemed to tear them apart.

"Stop fighting it, Arelan." Her voice cracked, but there was no emotion in it, only a quiet, painful resignation. "You don't know what's coming. You never did."

Arelan's eyes searched hers, but the woman he had known—the woman who had stood beside him, fought with him—wasn't there anymore. This was someone else. Someone different.

Althea stepped back, her hand brushing against the Emperor's as she returned to his side. It was a quiet, deliberate gesture. A silent acceptance.

The Emperor smiled, but it wasn't a smile of victory. It was a smile of understanding.

"You see," the Emperor said, his voice rising with the satisfaction of having laid everything bare, "the true power of the curse isn't in the Stone. It's in you—and in her. Together, you are the key to unlocking everything. A kingdom of shadows, built on magic, blood, and sacrifice."

Arelan felt the ground shift beneath him, the pull of the curse surging through him. He could feel Althea now, deep within his soul, her presence like a weight, like something that could never be torn away. They were connected in ways he hadn't

A Spell Between Shadows and Desire

known before, and the Stone—it had been right all along. It wasn't just a curse. It was the link. The bond.

"You both belong to me now," the Emperor said, stepping down from his throne, his eyes gleaming with a dark satisfaction. "You always have. You just didn't know it."

Arelan could feel the shadows closing in. They were his—the Emperor's shadows. They were his kingdom, his empire of power, blood, and death. He had created it, and now he was bringing them into it. The bond between Althea and Arelan was the key. They were part of the machine. Part of the plan.

Arelan's hands shook, and the dagger at his side felt heavier than ever. He wasn't sure if it was the curse or the rage that made it hard to breathe. He wasn't sure if it was Althea's betrayal or the Emperor's lies that made him want to tear everything apart.

But in that moment, something shifted within him. He couldn't let this stand. He couldn't let this kingdom of shadows take everything from him.

His hand tightened around the dagger.

"No." He whispered it at first, but then he said it louder. "No." His voice was steady, filled with a resolve that surprised even him.

The Emperor's smile faltered for just a moment. "You don't have a choice."

And Arelan knew that wasn't true. He had always had a choice. And now, with the power of the curse coursing through him, with the bond between him and Althea still tangled in ways he couldn't fully understand, he was about to make the one choice that would change everything.

It was time to tear down this kingdom of shadows.

Fourteen

The Last Sanctuary

The winds howled through the cracked stones, sweeping across the barren landscape like the breath of an ancient god. Arelan stood at the edge of the precipice, looking down at the vast expanse of nothingness that stretched out before him. The air here was different—sharp, heavy with the scent of magic and decay. It was a place that had once been a sanctuary, a refuge for those who sought peace in a world long consumed by darkness. But now, the sanctuary was no more. Now, it was a place of silence—a silence that felt suffocating, like the calm before a storm.

Arelan's fingers clenched around the hilt of his dagger, its familiar weight a steady reminder of the path he had chosen. The wind tugged at his cloak, and his breath came in ragged bursts, the cold air stinging his lungs. But it wasn't the chill that made his body tense. It was the weight of what lay ahead—the final confrontation, the culmination of everything that had brought him to this point.

Behind him, Althea stood still, her presence like a shadow at his back. The connection between them was undeniable, a bond forged in darkness, in blood, and in betrayal. And yet, it was the only thing that remained between them. The last thing that held them together in a world that seemed determined to tear them apart.

They had come this far. But how much further could they go?

Arelan's gaze flickered to Althea. She hadn't spoken since they had left the Emperor's palace. Since she had made her choice. Since she had turned her back on him—and, more importantly, on herself. Her face was pale, her eyes shadowed with a depth of sorrow that cut deeper than any weapon could.

"I thought you would understand," she whispered, her voice trembling, but her words were steady, as though she had already accepted what had happened. "I thought you would see it for what it was. A way out. For both of us."

Arelan closed his eyes, his chest tight. The truth had hit him hard when he realized she was the key, not just to the curse, but to everything that had led them here. The Emperor's game was far darker than he had ever imagined, and Althea—she had been a willing player. At least, that's what he had thought. But now, as he looked at her, he saw the truth of it. She hadn't wanted this. She had never wanted any of it. But the Stone had called to her, just as it had called to him. They had both been drawn into its power, its dark embrace.

"No," he said, his voice hoarse. "You wanted this. You chose this."

She didn't answer, but the look in her eyes—the way her shoulders slumped slightly as though she had been carrying an invisible weight—spoke volumes. She had never chosen him. She had chosen the Stone. She had chosen the power.

Arelan shook his head, a bitter laugh escaping his lips. "All this time. I thought—" His voice faltered. He didn't know what he thought anymore. Nothing seemed clear.

The wind gusted again, pulling at the hem of his cloak, and with it, something shifted in the air. A dark, oppressive weight settled over them, as though the very earth had drawn a breath, preparing for the worst. The ground beneath their feet seemed to tremble with anticipation.

"It's here," Althea said quietly, her gaze distant, as though she had already accepted what was coming. "The last sanctuary."

The words hung in the air like a grim prophecy, and Arelan felt a chill crawl up his spine. The Last Sanctuary was a place of legend, hidden deep within the heart of the empire, said to be the final refuge for those who had been touched by the dark forces. It was the one place the Emperor couldn't reach, the one place where the curse couldn't bind them.

But was it truly a sanctuary? Or was it merely another trap?

The Last Sanctuary

Arelan turned away from Althea, his eyes scanning the desolate horizon. In the distance, beyond the crumbling ruins of the old city, the silhouette of the sanctuary rose like a ghost from the ashes. The towering spires were dark, the stone gleaming faintly in the dim light of the setting sun. It was a place of power, a place of ancient magic, and a place that held the last hope of breaking the chains that bound them.

But it was also a place of danger.

Arelan knew that. And yet, there was no other choice. They had come this far. There was no turning back now.

Without another word, he began to walk toward the sanctuary, his boots crunching on the frost-covered ground. Althea followed him, her steps hesitant, but she didn't speak. She didn't need to. They both knew what was at stake. They both knew what they had to do. But would they be able to break the curse that had held them for so long? Could they free themselves from the Emperor's clutches? Or would they fall to the same darkness that had consumed everything they had ever known?

The wind picked up again, howling through the empty landscape as they approached the gates of the sanctuary. The air grew colder, the shadows deepening with every step they took. Arelan's hand gripped the hilt of his dagger tightly, the cold metal pressing against his palm like a reminder of everything he had lost.

When they reached the gates, Althea stopped. Her fingers

brushed against the cold stone, and for a moment, Arelan saw something flicker in her eyes—an emotion he couldn't place, something like fear, but deeper than that. Her breath came in short bursts, her chest rising and falling as though she were trying to steady herself.

"I never wanted this," she said again, her voice barely audible. "I never wanted any of this."

Arelan turned to her, his heart heavy with a mixture of regret and understanding. He knew now that her betrayal hadn't been about power. It hadn't been about him. It had been about survival. The Stone had promised freedom, a way out of the Emperor's grip. But the price had been too high.

"Althea…" His voice was quiet, but it was filled with something more than just sorrow. It was a plea. A plea for her to see the truth. To see that they could still break free, together.

But she only shook her head, her eyes hardening again. "No, Arelan. We can't. The curse has bound us. There's no way out."

With that, she pushed open the gates of the sanctuary, the heavy doors creaking as they groaned on their hinges. The darkness beyond them stretched out like an abyss, and for a moment, Arelan hesitated. He could feel it—the weight of the decision pressing down on him. Once they crossed that threshold, there would be no turning back. They would be committed, bound to whatever fate awaited them inside.

But it was too late to second-guess himself now.

The Last Sanctuary

He stepped forward.

The moment they crossed the threshold, the world seemed to shift. The air became heavier, charged with a strange energy, as though the very fabric of reality had bent to their will. The ancient magic of the sanctuary hummed beneath their feet, resonating with the power that had always been a part of Arelan, a part of them.

But it wasn't just the magic that caught his attention. It was the voices—whispers in the air, faint at first, but growing louder with every step they took. Arelan's pulse quickened as the voices began to swirl around them, a cacophony of words that seemed to come from all directions.

The walls of the sanctuary pulsed with a life of their own, the ancient stone groaning under the weight of the power contained within. It was a place of secrets, a place of lost magic, but it wasn't just a refuge. It was a prison. And Arelan could feel the presence of something far older, far darker, lying in wait.

Althea reached out, her hand trembling as it brushed against the stone walls. "We're not alone," she said, her voice shaking with the weight of her words.

Arelan nodded. "I know."

They were far deeper in the sanctuary now, the light from outside growing dimmer with every step. And as they moved forward, the whispers grew louder, more insistent. It was as though the sanctuary itself was alive, pulling them in, testing them.

And then, suddenly, the stone beneath their feet shifted. A loud crack reverberated through the sanctuary, and the floor beneath them split open, revealing a hidden chamber deep below. The darkness seemed to swallow them whole as they stared down into the abyss.

Arelan felt the cold sweat bead on his brow. This was it. This was the moment where everything would either be lost or won. The fate of everything—of the curse, of the Stone, of Althea and him—rested on what happened next.

He turned to Althea, his eyes searching hers. The bond between them was undeniable, but there was still something between them, something unspoken. Could they truly break free from the curse? Could they undo what had been done?

"We go together," he said quietly, his voice resolute.

And with that, they stepped forward, into the abyss.

Fifteen

A Desperate Bargain

The air in the hidden chamber of the sanctuary was thick with the scent of damp earth and decay. The moment Arelan and Althea descended into the cavernous depths, a strange weight pressed down on them, an oppressive force that seemed to make the very walls close in around them. The torchlight flickered weakly as if the flame itself were reluctant to burn, the shadows around them deepening with every step they took.

Arelan's heart raced, each beat louder than the last, drowning out the whispers that had followed them into the sanctuary. He could still feel the pull of the curse, thrumming beneath his skin, trying to seize control of his every movement. The bond between him and Althea, forged in darkness and tempered with betrayal, was still there, an invisible thread that connected them even now.

They had reached the heart of the sanctuary—the last place the Emperor had feared to touch, the last place where the dark magic of the Severing Stone could truly be undone. But as they approached the center of the cavern, the weight of the magic in the air became unbearable. It pressed down on Arelan's chest, making it hard to breathe, hard to think. It felt as though the very earth beneath them was alive, pulsating with ancient power, with secrets long buried and forgotten.

The stone altar in the center of the chamber was bathed in an eerie, soft light, its surface etched with symbols that seemed to shimmer and shift as they drew near. The air around it hummed with energy, a low vibration that seemed to resonate with the very bones of Arelan's body. He could feel the Stone's presence—its hunger, its power—reaching out to him. It knew he was here. It knew they were here.

Althea's voice broke through his thoughts, soft, almost tentative. "This is it, Arelan. The heart of the Stone's power. The place where it all began."

Her words felt like a spell, wrapping around him, drawing him deeper into the web of fate that had already ensnared them both. The power in this place was undeniable, and as much as Arelan wanted to deny it, he knew that it was only a matter of time before they would have to confront it—and the choices they had made.

"We can't turn back," Arelan said, his voice rough, his throat tight as though something inside him were choking him, refusing to let him speak freely. The weight of the moment pressed in on him, making every word feel like it cost him something. "There's no escape from this."

Althea turned to face him, her eyes dark with something he couldn't read. She opened her mouth, but before she could speak, a sharp, sudden noise broke the silence—a low growl, almost imperceptible, but it was there, lurking in the shadows. Arelan tensed, instinctively reaching for his dagger, but his body felt sluggish, the curse inside him demanding his attention, urging him to stop fighting, to embrace it.

"Something's wrong," Althea whispered, her voice barely audible above the growl that echoed in the cavern. "I can feel it."

Arelan turned his head sharply, his eyes scanning the dark corners of the chamber, trying to find the source of the noise, the threat that loomed unseen. The shadows twisted, contorted, as if something were moving beneath them, shifting just out of sight.

Suddenly, the air around them thickened, the temperature dropping drastically. A chill ran down Arelan's spine, his breath misting in front of him as the growl grew louder. It was no longer a sound—it was a presence. Something ancient. Something hungry.

A voice—low, guttural—spoke from the darkness.

"You think you can destroy it? The Stone, the curse—it is beyond your reach. You cannot change what is fated."

The voice seemed to come from everywhere at once, surrounding them, seeping into their minds, drowning out everything else. Arelan's breath caught in his throat as the figure materialized from the shadows.

It was him.

The Emperor.

But this wasn't the man he had seen before, seated upon his throne, cold and distant. This was something else—a twisted, spectral version of the Emperor, his eyes burning with an unnatural light, his form flickering like a shadow in the dark. He stepped forward, his movements smooth and fluid, but there was something wrong about him—his very presence seemed to warp the air around him, distorting the space they stood in.

"Althea," the Emperor's voice rumbled, "you think you can escape your destiny? You think you can change the course of fate itself?"

Arelan's hand tightened around the dagger. He could feel the curse surging through him, pushing him to act, but he held it back. He couldn't let the Emperor control him—not now. Not after everything that had happened.

Althea's voice shook as she stepped forward, her hand reaching toward the Emperor's form. "You—what have you done to us? What is this? Why did you make us this way?"

The Emperor's spectral form tilted its head, its hollow eyes

A Desperate Bargain

glimmering with malicious delight. "I didn't make you this way, Althea. You chose it. You both chose it. The curse, the Stone, the bond—this was always your fate. You have always been destined to be bound together. And now, you will serve your purpose."

Arelan's chest tightened as the words sank in. The Emperor was right, in a twisted way. The curse that bound him and Althea together was more than just a trap. It was a design—a plan, centuries in the making. The power of the Severing Stone wasn't just about breaking curses. It was about control. It was about enslaving them to a will far greater than their own.

"Why?" Arelan's voice was barely a whisper. "Why use us like this?"

The Emperor's laugh was low, cold, and filled with dark amusement. "Because you were always meant to be tools—weapons to be wielded. And you," he said, turning his gaze to Althea, "you were always the key. The power that was bound within you from the very beginning."

Althea's face paled, her fingers trembling at her sides. She opened her mouth, but no words came out. The Emperor's presence was suffocating, his power pressing down on them like a weight that couldn't be escaped.

Arelan stepped forward, his fists clenched. "You're lying. This isn't us. This isn't our fate."

The Emperor's form flickered again, a cruel smile spreading

across his face. "Do you truly believe you have a choice? The curse binds you. The Stone binds you. You belong to me, Arelan. And you," he added, his gaze turning to Althea, "you belong to the empire. Together, you will serve a greater purpose. You will break the chains of your past, and you will usher in the reign of the true rulers of this world."

Althea stepped back, her breath ragged. Arelan could see the struggle within her—her fear, her anger, her confusion. She had been a part of this, a part of the Emperor's grand design, but now, in the face of the truth, she didn't know how to fight it. The weight of the power inside her was suffocating, and yet she had never wanted it. Never asked for it.

"We won't be your slaves," Althea finally said, her voice gaining strength as she looked the Emperor dead in the eye. "We won't serve you."

The Emperor's smile faded, replaced by a cold, calculating expression. "Very well. If you will not serve willingly, then I will make you."

Before Arelan could react, the Emperor raised his hand, and the shadows around them erupted, a tidal wave of darkness crashing over them. Arelan felt it before he saw it—the curse—writhing, pushing against him like a physical force, threatening to overtake him. The power inside him surged, but it wasn't his own. It was the Emperor's magic, laced with the curse, pushing him, controlling him.

He stumbled, his knees buckling as the magic pressed against

A Desperate Bargain

him. It felt as if the Stone itself were pulling at him, trying to draw him into its depths, to devour him whole.

But Althea—she wasn't frozen. She moved.

With a sudden, explosive force, she reached toward the Emperor. Her hand glowed with a fierce, white light—pure, untainted magic. The Emperor's form faltered for a moment, his dark energy recoiling from her as she unleashed the power within her.

"I will not be your puppet," Althea said, her voice ringing with defiance.

Arelan struggled to move, his body still under the Emperor's control. He could feel the power surging within her, the light that burned through the darkness. She was fighting it. Fighting him.

And in that moment, Arelan understood. They were bound together, not just by the curse, but by something stronger. Hope.

With everything he had left, he reached for her, his hand trembling as he grabbed her wrist. Together, they could break the chains. Together, they could defy the Emperor.

The bond between them surged, and the Stone itself seemed to respond, its power bending to their will.

And for the first time in what felt like forever, Arelan felt the chains begin to break.

Sixteen

The Assassin's Heart

The air was thick with the scent of blood and smoke as Arelan stumbled through the crumbling halls of the sanctuary, his body trembling, his mind on the verge of collapse. The Emperor's power had been overwhelming, its darkness nearly suffocating, but in the end, they had managed to break through—Althea and him, together. The Emperor's hold on them had finally loosened, the curse weakening with each passing moment. But even now, as they moved through the shadows, the weight of everything that had happened still pressed on Arelan, pulling him down into the depths of his own turmoil.

He had always known that he was a weapon—an instrument of death, forged by the hands of those who sought to control him. But what he hadn't realized, until now, was that he had never truly been free. Not until he had met Althea. Not until he had fought beside her. She had been his anchor, his strength. But now... now he didn't know what he had left.

The sanctuary was no longer a place of refuge. It was a tomb. The walls that had once whispered of ancient magic now seemed to scream with the weight of lost souls, each step they took reverberating through the cold stone, each breath they drew a reminder of everything they had lost. The light from their torches cast long, flickering shadows that seemed to chase them, pushing them forward, deeper into the heart of the ruins.

Arelan's hand instinctively reached for his dagger, but it wasn't there. He had left it behind in the chaos, its weight a distant memory now. He didn't need it. Not anymore. The curse that had once bound him to the blade had faded, but in its place was something else—something darker, more insidious.

Althea walked beside him, her face pale, her expression unreadable. He could feel the tension between them, thick and unspoken, the air heavy with the weight of their shared past. The bond that had once felt like a lifeline now felt like a chain, pulling them in opposite directions.

"Are you all right?" Arelan's voice was hoarse, the words barely a whisper, but they felt like a breaking point, like a line he wasn't sure he wanted to cross.

Althea didn't answer immediately. She kept walking, her eyes fixed ahead, her steps steady but slow. He knew her well enough to know that she was running from something. Maybe from him. Maybe from herself.

"I'm fine," she said, her voice flat, distant. But even as she said the words, Arelan could see the tremble in her hands, the tightness in her shoulders. She was anything but fine.

"You're not fine," Arelan pressed, his voice sharper now. "You've been carrying this weight for far too long. And so have I." He stopped walking, turning to face her. "We don't have to do this alone, Althea. We never did."

Her gaze met his, and for a moment, there was something in her eyes—something raw, something unguarded. The walls she had so carefully built around herself were beginning to crack, just a little. She looked at him as though she were seeing him for the first time, as though the man standing before her was no longer the assassin who had once been bound to a blade, but someone else entirely.

"I don't know who I am anymore," Althea whispered, her voice breaking. "I've spent so long pretending that I knew what I was doing. That I had control over my choices, over my fate. But I was wrong."

Arelan felt his heart clench at her words, the truth of them cutting deeper than any blade ever could. "We both were," he said quietly. "But it's not too late, Althea. We can still change this. We can still find a way to break the curse for good. Together."

Althea looked away, her eyes searching the darkness of the sanctuary as if it held the answers she so desperately needed. "I don't know if I can believe that anymore," she said, her voice barely above a whisper. "I don't know if I can believe in us."

The words hit him like a physical blow. Arelan had always known that their bond was fragile, but hearing her say it out loud, hearing the doubt in her voice, made him realize just how much they had both been through—how much they had lost.

"You don't have to believe in us, Althea," Arelan said, stepping closer to her, his voice softer now, almost pleading. "But you have to believe in you. You've always been stronger than you think. And I'm not giving up on you. I'm not giving up on us."

Her eyes flickered with something—a flicker of hope, perhaps, or maybe just the ghosts of memories they had once shared. She met his gaze, her expression unreadable, and for a moment, it seemed as though she might say something. But before she could speak, the air around them shifted.

A sharp, almost tangible crackle filled the air, the temperature dropping as the ground beneath them trembled. The sanctuary seemed to come alive with a dark energy, the walls groaning with the weight of ancient magic. Arelan's hand shot out, grabbing Althea's wrist, pulling her back as the ground began to crack and split open.

The world around them shook violently, the stone beneath their feet cracking open like a wound, dark shadows spilling from the cracks. The air was thick with a terrible, suffocating magic, and Arelan's heart skipped a beat as the realization hit him: They weren't alone.

A figure emerged from the shadows, its shape barely visible in the dim light, but the presence of it was undeniable. The darkness seemed to bend around the figure like a shroud, its form moving with an unnatural grace, its eyes glowing with an eerie, greenish light.

The Emperor.

Arelan's blood ran cold. It couldn't be. They had destroyed him. They had broken his hold on them. But there he stood, his form flickering in and out of existence, as though he were nothing more than a ghost, a shadow of the man he once was.

"You thought you could escape me," the Emperor's voice echoed, deep and resonant, a sound that seemed to come from everywhere and nowhere at once. "But the curse is never truly broken. It binds you, Arelan. And it binds her."

Arelan's breath caught in his throat. The Emperor's words felt like a hammer to his chest. He had known, in his darkest moments, that there was no escaping the curse. But this—this—this was something else entirely. The Emperor had never been gone. He had never truly left them.

"You will never be free," the Emperor continued, his voice a low, menacing growl. "This sanctuary is not what it seems. It is but a prison, a cage for those who seek to escape the inevitable. And you—" His gaze locked onto Althea, "—are the key to the final piece of the puzzle."

Arelan stepped forward, his body trembling with a mixture of fear and rage. "You won't control us anymore. You won't—"

But the Emperor raised his hand, silencing him with a single motion. The shadows around them grew darker, denser, until they seemed to swallow the light from their torches. Arelan felt it again—the curse, the darkness surging through his veins, wrapping around his soul like iron chains.

"You never had control," the Emperor hissed. "Neither of you. The curse was always meant to bring you to me. To this place. To this moment."

The ground trembled again, and Arelan stumbled as the walls of the sanctuary began to close in, the stone shifting, grinding, as if the very structure of the world were beginning to tear itself apart. Althea cried out, her body convulsing as the power of the Emperor's magic took hold of her, pulling her toward him.

"No!" Arelan shouted, reaching for her, but it was too late.

The Emperor's hand extended, his fingers crackling with dark energy. Althea's body jerked toward him, her face contorted with pain, but she didn't resist. She couldn't.

The bond between them—the curse, the Stone—was stronger than either of them had realized.

"Arelan…" Althea gasped, her voice weak, her eyes filled with something far worse than fear. It was regret. "I'm sorry… I never wanted this… I never wanted to be… this."

The Assassin's Heart

The Emperor's laughter echoed in the chamber, a cruel, mocking sound that shattered Arelan's heart. He couldn't lose her. He couldn't let her fall back into the darkness.

His dagger, forgotten and abandoned at his side, was now the only thing that could break the curse. The only thing that could sever the bond that tied them to the Emperor's will.

But as he reached for it, the Emperor's power surged again, sending a wave of energy crashing into him. Arelan's body convulsed, his mind slipping as the darkness wrapped itself around his thoughts.

He could feel the presence of the Emperor in his mind, deep inside, pulling at his will, urging him to submit, to surrender.

But he couldn't.

Not now. Not after everything they had been through.

With every ounce of strength left in him, Arelan fought back.

And the dagger came free.

Seventeen

A Spell Between Shadows and Desire

The ground beneath Arelan's feet shook violently, as though the very earth itself had grown restless. The sanctuary was no longer the place of refuge it had once seemed—no, now it was a tomb, an arena for a final battle that neither of them could escape. The air was thick with a cold, suffocating magic, swirling like a storm of shadows. Althea was still before him, her form trembling as she fought against the Emperor's dark influence, but it wasn't just the power that held her—it was the connection between them, the unspoken bond that had been forged by the curse, by the Stone, and by their shared history. The curse had always been more than just magic—it had been a thread, drawing them closer together with every passing day, binding them until it seemed there was no distinction between their hearts, no space between their souls.

A Spell Between Shadows and Desire

Arelan's fingers clenched around the dagger at his side, the cold metal biting into his palm. He could feel it, the weight of the world pressing down on him, the burden of every decision that had led him here, to this moment. He could feel the rage boiling within him, the desire to end this—to end the Emperor's grip on them, to free them both. But at the same time, there was something else—something darker. It was the curse, the power within him, pulling him toward Althea. Toward her.

She was still standing, struggling to keep her footing as the Emperor's magic twisted around her like invisible chains. Her face was pale, her eyes locked on the Emperor's spectral form, but there was something in her gaze—a flicker of uncertainty, of fear—that made Arelan's heart ache. She was torn, caught between the power that had claimed her and the desire to break free.

And as much as Arelan wanted to blame her for everything—the betrayal, the lies, the darkness that had consumed them both—he couldn't. He couldn't because he knew. He knew that they had both been caught in a web spun long ago, a web that was now unraveling before them.

"Althea," he said, his voice hoarse, filled with a raw desperation. "Fight it. You can't let him control you any longer."

Her eyes flickered toward him, but she didn't speak. There was a hardness to her gaze, a barrier that he couldn't breach. The Emperor's power still held her, and Arelan could feel it too, tugging at his own will, pushing him to submit. But there was something in him—something deep down—that refused to give in.

The Emperor's laughter echoed through the chamber, a deep, mocking sound that made Arelan's blood run cold. "You think you can defy me?" the Emperor's voice rang out, smooth and serpentine. "You think you can break the curse? The bond between you two is unbreakable. It has always been unbreakable. The Stone is the key to everything. And you—" He turned his cold, burning gaze on Arelan, "—you are nothing but a tool, a weapon forged for my use. You are mine. And she—she always was."

Arelan's heart pounded in his chest. The words stung, but they didn't break him. He had always known that he had been a pawn in the Emperor's game, a weapon used by the very man who had cursed him. But now—now it was different. He wasn't just fighting for his freedom. He was fighting for her—for the woman he had once trusted, for the woman who had stood by him, even when everything seemed impossible. He couldn't let the Emperor take her again. He wouldn't.

"Shut up," Arelan growled, his voice thick with anger. He stepped forward, his eyes locked on the Emperor's form. "You don't know anything. You don't understand what she means to me."

The Emperor's eyes gleamed with amusement. "Oh, but I do," he said, his tone cold and condescending. "I know her better than you ever could. You see, she has always been the key. Always the one who could unlock the power of the Stone, who could control its magic. You were just a tool. A temporary distraction."

Althea's hands trembled at her sides, and Arelan could see the strain in her eyes. She was trying to fight, trying to break free, but the Emperor's power was like a vice around her, squeezing, pulling at the very fabric of her will.

"No!" Arelan shouted, his voice breaking through the suffocating air. "You won't control us anymore. Not like this."

He looked at Althea, his eyes filled with something desperate. Something more than just desire. "Please," he whispered, his voice hoarse. "Let me help you. Let me save you."

Althea's eyes softened for just a moment, but the Emperor's power twisted in the air, and she gasped, as though something had torn at her soul. She staggered, her body shaking with the strain of the magic that held her, but she didn't fall.

The Emperor's form loomed over them, its presence growing darker, more oppressive. "You think you can fight destiny? You think you can break the bond?" His voice was a low, menacing growl, the shadows swirling around him like an extension of his will. "The Stone is our destiny. You were never meant to escape."

Arelan's chest tightened as the curse surged within him. He could feel the shadows reaching for him, pulling at him, twisting him with its power. But even in the face of it, he could feel something else—a flicker of light, a flicker of hope—coming from Althea. It was the only thing he had left. The only thing that mattered.

He stepped forward, his hand reaching out toward her. "Althea," he said, his voice steady, despite the storm of power swirling around them. "You are stronger than this. We can fight this. We can break free together."

For a moment, there was silence. The world around them seemed to still, the air thick with anticipation. Arelan's heart raced as he looked at her, his breath shallow, his mind spinning. He didn't know if it was the curse or the bond between them, but for the first time, he truly felt the weight of what they were about to do. The stakes were higher than ever before.

Then, Althea moved.

With a strength Arelan hadn't seen in her before, she stepped toward him. Her hand reached out, trembling, but determined. And as she touched his hand, a spark of light erupted between them—a surge of magic, pure and untainted, that broke through the darkness.

The Emperor's form recoiled, his eyes flashing with fury. "No!" he screamed, his voice cracking with the force of the magic that suddenly began to unravel his hold on them. "You cannot defy me! You are mine!"

But Arelan felt the pull of the Stone weaken, the curse loosening its grip on him. He could feel it in his very bones, the magic that had once bound him to the Emperor—to Althea—beginning to dissolve, like smoke in the wind.

Together, they were stronger than the curse. Stronger than the Emperor.

The darkness around them surged, but Arelan didn't falter. He looked at Althea, his heart racing in his chest. Her eyes met his, and for the first time, he saw something there—a flicker of love. A flicker of trust.

And in that moment, they both understood.

They had spent so long running from their past, from the curse, from the bond between them. But now, they weren't running. Now, they were standing together, facing it head-on. They had the power to break it.

They had the power to destroy it.

With a final, unified effort, they raised their hands toward the Emperor, the light between them growing brighter, more intense, until the very air crackled with the power they had unleashed. The Stone pulsed once more, but this time, it was no longer a threat. It was a beacon—a force of magic that resonated through them both, uniting them in a way nothing else ever could.

The Emperor screamed, his form disintegrating into nothingness as the light from the Stone tore through the darkness that had surrounded them for so long. Arelan could feel it—the curse, the power, the bond—breaking apart, shattering into a thousand fragments, each one dissolving into the wind.

And in that moment, Arelan realized something he had never known before.

The power between them, the curse, the magic—it wasn't about control. It wasn't about dominance. It was about choice. The choice to stand together. To fight together. To break the chains that had once bound them.

And as the last remnants of the Emperor's influence crumbled away, leaving nothing but a silence that felt somehow freeing, Arelan knew that this—this was the beginning of something new.

Something they could finally call their own.

With Althea by his side, he no longer felt like a weapon. No longer felt like a tool to be used and discarded. He felt like a man.

And together, they would face whatever came next.

Eighteen

The Fall of an Empire

The ground trembled beneath Arelan's feet, as though the very foundations of the world were shaking in the aftermath of everything that had transpired. The echoes of the Emperor's final scream still rang in his ears, the dark energy that had once bound him to the curse now vanishing into the wind. He could feel the weight of it—the end of a story that had been written for them both long before they had ever known it. But now, the world around them was changing. Everything was shifting. And Arelan didn't know what came next.

The sanctuary was quiet, eerily so, but the stillness wasn't comforting. It was as though the entire realm was holding its breath, waiting for the next move, the next chapter in a war that had been raging for centuries. The Emperor was gone, his reign shattered, but the empire he had created—the one that had shaped their lives, their fates—was still very much alive.

And now, it was crumbling.

Arelan stood in the heart of the sanctuary, his chest tight with the weight of it all. He could still feel the echoes of the curse within him, like a fading shadow in the corners of his mind, but it was weaker now. They had destroyed it. The Stone had no more hold on him. No more control.

Beside him, Althea moved silently, her steps slow and measured as she looked around the chamber. The light that had erupted when they shattered the Emperor's power still lingered in the air, casting long shadows across the ruins of the sanctuary. Her face was a mask, unreadable, but Arelan could see the faint tremor in her hands—the aftershocks of the battle they had just fought. She, too, was struggling to come to terms with what they had done.

"What now?" Arelan asked, his voice breaking the silence. His words felt like a rupture in the air, a crack in the calm after the storm.

Althea didn't look at him immediately. She took a slow step toward the altar, her gaze drawn to the remnants of the power that had been unleashed. The Stone, once a source of unyielding darkness, now lay shattered at the base of the altar, its once-glowing surface dull and lifeless.

"I don't know," Althea whispered, her voice distant. "The Emperor is gone. The curse is gone. But the world he created…

it doesn't end with him."

Arelan frowned, his gaze moving to the farthest corners of the sanctuary. He could still feel the tremors in the air, the faint remnants of power lingering like smoke after a fire. The echoes of the Emperor's presence were still here, woven into the fabric of the empire itself. This place—the sanctuary—had once been a refuge, but now it felt like a tomb, a memorial to everything they had lost.

"But his empire is still standing," Arelan said, his voice hardening. "And it's falling apart from the inside. His people. His army. His alliances… they're all going to collapse without him."

Althea's face remained calm, but Arelan could see the faintest flicker of something in her eyes. Something like guilt. Or fear. "I'm not the one who can stop it, Arelan. You know that."

He turned to face her, his eyes narrowing. "I'm not the one who's going to rebuild it either."

The words hung in the air between them, sharp and biting, like shards of glass. There had been a time, not so long ago, when he might have believed in the idea of rebuilding. A time when he thought that, together, they could change the world, reshape it, fix the broken pieces of the empire the Emperor had left behind. But now—now it felt impossible.

"It's not about rebuilding it," Arelan said, his voice softer now, tinged with something he hadn't expected. "It's about destroying it. Completely."

Althea looked at him then, and for the first time since the Emperor's defeat, their eyes met in silence. There was no anger between them. No tension. Just the raw weight of everything they had been through—the betrayals, the struggles, the wars fought and lost.

But beneath that weight, beneath the shadows of the past, something else was stirring. Something new.

"We can't just leave it like this," Althea said, her voice steady, but there was an edge to it now, a hint of resolve that had been missing before. "We can't let what he built continue, even if he's gone."

Arelan nodded, understanding. He felt it too—the call to action. The world they had fought so hard to escape, the empire that had tried to control them, was still alive. The soldiers, the officials, the puppet rulers who had been loyal to the Emperor—they were still out there. And without their leader, they would turn on each other, fighting for scraps, for power.

But they didn't have to be part of it anymore. They could end it. They could bring the empire to its knees.

"You're right," Arelan said, stepping toward her. "We can't leave it to rot. We can't let the bloodshed continue. We have to end it all."

Althea's gaze softened, but her resolve remained firm. "But it's not just the empire, Arelan. It's the people. The ones who've been deceived. The ones who don't know any better. We can't just wipe it out and leave the pieces to fall apart."

The words hit him harder than he expected. He had always seen the empire as something to destroy, something to fight against. But Althea was right. The people—the innocent people—had been caught in the same web, trapped by the same curse, the same lies.

"How do we do it?" Arelan asked, his voice barely above a whisper.

Althea turned toward the altar, her expression unreadable. She stepped closer, her fingers brushing against the remnants of the Stone. "We don't destroy it all at once. We take it apart piece by piece. We break the foundations."

Arelan's heart pounded as he understood what she was saying. "You want to take the power back. You want to make the people see the truth."

She nodded, her gaze distant. "We have to show them the reality of the Empire. Not just the Emperor, but the entire system. The corruption, the manipulation. We tear it down from the inside."

Arelan's chest tightened with a mix of emotions. It wasn't just about destruction—it was about rebirth. It was about the people. About the future. He couldn't believe he hadn't seen it before. The rebellion, the fight, had never just been about breaking free from the Emperor. It had always been about giving the people the power to make their own choices, to take back what had been stolen from them.

"I can't do it alone," Althea said, turning to him. "Neither can you."

Arelan looked at her, his heart heavy with the weight of what they had to do. But for the first time, the path ahead seemed clear. They had fought the Emperor. They had broken the curse. Now, they had to fight for something bigger—something worth living for.

"We won't be alone," Arelan said softly. "We'll find the others. The ones who still believe. The ones who want to see the Empire fall."

"And when it does," Althea replied, her voice strong, "we'll rebuild it. But this time, it will be on our terms. Not theirs."

Arelan stepped forward, closing the distance between them. Their eyes met again, but this time, there was no hesitation. No walls between them. It was as if everything that had kept them apart—the betrayals, the lies, the curse—had faded, leaving only the truth. And that truth was simple.

They were in this together.

"We'll burn it down," Arelan whispered, his voice filled with a renewed sense of purpose. "And we'll rise from the ashes."

As the words left his lips, the air in the sanctuary shifted, a low hum filling the space as though the world itself had just begun to turn. Outside the sanctuary, the world was still waiting. The empire, broken and crumbling, was about to feel the weight of its own fall.

And Arelan, with Althea by his side, would make sure it would never rise again.

The first light of dawn broke through the cracks in the stone, casting a new light on the ruins. They had one chance to change everything. To rebuild. To start again.

Together.

Nineteen

A Love That Defies Fate

The world felt strangely silent as Arelan and Althea stepped away from the shattered remnants of the Stone. The sanctuary's once-ancient walls, drenched in the blood of the past, now seemed like a hollow memory of a time that had been wiped away. The air, heavy with the remains of dark magic and ancient curses, felt lighter, like the earth had taken a long, deep breath. The Emperor was gone, his power disintegrating with every heartbeat, but the world they knew—the world shaped by his twisted hand—still loomed before them.

And yet, amidst the broken stone and fading magic, something remained between them. A connection stronger than the curse that had once bound them. Stronger than the betrayals they had endured. A love, perhaps, but something more. It was a defiance. A defiance that had brought them here, to this moment, when the world had been reset, where the very air seemed to tremble with the possibility of something new.

But this wasn't just about destroying the Emperor's empire. It wasn't even about breaking the chains of magic that had bound them together. It was about them—about choosing each other, choosing a future that could still be theirs, no matter the cost.

Arelan's eyes were fixed on Althea, who stood a few steps away from him, her back straight and her gaze distant. Her face was as pale as it had been when they had first entered the sanctuary, but now, there was something else in her—something stronger than the fear, stronger than the shadow of doubt. It was determination. Hope.

Her breath was steady as she looked at him, but there was a tightness around her mouth that suggested she was holding something back, something she wasn't yet ready to say. He could feel it in the air between them—the weight of everything they had been through, everything they had survived. The love that had been torn apart by lies, by betrayal, by the very magic that had sought to control them, was still there.

But the world around them—the ruins of the Emperor's empire—was still waiting. Still watching. And Arelan knew that if they were to ever have a chance at happiness, at peace, they would have to face it all, together.

"Althea," Arelan said, his voice low and steady, cutting through the stillness of the sanctuary. "We're not done. Not yet."

She turned toward him then, her eyes meeting his for the first time since they had left the Emperor's presence. The silence between them was almost unbearable, but there was an understanding in the way she looked at him, as if she knew exactly what he meant. They couldn't just walk away. They had to finish this.

Her lips parted, and for a moment, Arelan thought she might say something else—something final. But instead, her voice was quiet, almost broken. "What if it's too late? What if the damage is too great to undo?"

Arelan took a step closer, his hand reaching for hers. The world outside had been shattered. The Emperor's reign was over, but the pieces of the world they had known were still scattered in a thousand different directions. The empire was crumbling, the people lost in the chaos, and the power of the curse—the darkness that had been planted in the hearts of men—wasn't just something they could erase. It had to be destroyed, piece by piece. They had to make the people see the truth, show them what had been built on the bones of the innocent.

"It's not too late," Arelan replied, his voice firm. "We're not the only ones who want to see this end. You said it yourself—people can still change. They can still choose. But we have to lead them."

He saw the flicker of uncertainty in her eyes, but there was something else, too—a flicker of understanding. She stepped closer to him, her hand finding his.

"I don't know if I can ever forgive myself for what I've done," she said, her voice soft, barely a whisper. "For the choices I made. For the people I hurt."

Arelan's heart tightened at the words. He knew the pain she was feeling. He had lived through it himself. But that was the curse of fate—that it always made them pay, always made them carry the weight of their choices, even if they had never truly been given a choice at all.

"You don't need to forgive yourself," he said, his voice rough with emotion. "We can't undo the past, Althea. But we can choose how to move forward. Together."

For a long moment, neither of them spoke. They were alone in the world now. The Emperor was gone, but the empire's destruction was only just beginning. It was a kingdom built on shadows, and the people who had lived in those shadows were lost, broken, confused. They had to help them find their way. They had to rebuild.

Arelan reached out, gently cupping her face in his hands, his thumb brushing across her cheek. The touch was soft, tender, and it felt like a promise. A promise that no matter how far they had fallen, no matter how broken the world had become, they could still rebuild it. Together.

"You and I," he whispered, his breath shaky. "We've been through hell. And we survived. We can survive this too. We can find a way to rebuild, Althea. A way to make them see the truth. To tear down the lies and the darkness."

She closed her eyes at his words, and for a moment, Arelan thought she might say something—some final words of doubt or resignation. But when she opened her eyes again, there was something different in them. A glimmer of hope. Of belief. Of trust.

"I don't know if I can lead them," she said softly, her voice trembling. "I don't know if they'll follow me."

Arelan stepped back, taking her hands in his, feeling the warmth of her skin against his. "You don't have to lead them alone," he said firmly. "You never have to do it alone."

The ground around them began to shake again, but this time, it wasn't the power of the Emperor's curse. This time, it was the force of a world that was beginning to shift, the world that they had chosen to fight for. The people were out there, scattered, fractured, but they were still there. And they would fight alongside them. They would rebuild together.

"I don't know what will happen," Althea whispered, looking up at him with uncertain eyes, but there was something else there now, something that had been missing for so long— determination. "But I'm not going to run anymore. I'm going to stand with you, Arelan. I'm going to fight for them."

Arelan's heart swelled with a mix of relief and joy. He had always known that she was strong, that she had the power to change the world, but it was more than that. It was her. Her strength. Her heart. She wasn't the same woman who had walked into the sanctuary so long ago, filled with uncertainty and fear. She was someone new, someone forged in the fire of their shared pain, their shared battle.

"I'll fight for you, Althea," he said, his voice unwavering. "We'll rebuild. Not just the empire, but the people. We'll give them the truth. We'll give them hope."

The air around them shifted again, and this time, it was with purpose. The ground beneath their feet rumbled, but this time, it felt different. It felt like the beginning of something. Not the end. Not destruction. But rebirth.

They turned together, stepping forward into the unknown. The road ahead was uncertain, filled with danger and doubt, but it was also filled with possibility. They were no longer bound by the chains of the past. The curse had been broken. The Emperor was gone. And now, the world was theirs to shape.

Together, they would build something new. Something better.

And as they walked forward into the future, side by side, the shadows that had once chased them seemed to retreat, replaced by the first light of dawn.

For the first time in their lives, they were free.

And this time, they would choose their own fate.

Twenty

Whispers Beyond the Veil

The moon hung high over the broken ruins, casting long, jagged shadows that seemed to stretch across the land like the fingers of something ancient. The night air was cool, but it carried with it a sense of something unfinished, something lingering in the corners of the world that refused to be silenced. Arelan stood at the edge of the remnants of the sanctuary, his eyes scanning the vast, desolate landscape before him. The world had changed, yes, but there were still pieces missing—pieces that needed to be found, truths that needed to be uncovered.

He turned, his gaze finding Althea standing a few steps behind him. Her silhouette was bathed in the pale moonlight, her face shadowed, but the determination in her stance was as clear as the night sky. They had won. They had shattered the curse, ended the Emperor's reign, and yet, the weight of the victory felt strangely hollow. The world they had freed was still broken, the empire in ruins, and the people lost in the aftermath.

Althea had been silent for the better part of the evening, her thoughts consumed by the same weight that seemed to hang over Arelan. They had chosen to stand against the Emperor together, but now, there was something new between them. Something unfamiliar. The world had changed, but so had they. They weren't just survivors anymore—they were something different, something more. And yet, there was a distance between them now, an unspoken tension that neither of them knew how to address.

"Do you hear it?" Althea's voice broke the silence, soft and uncertain, but it held something else in it—a trace of fear. She wasn't looking at him now. Her eyes were focused somewhere beyond the ruins, into the darkened horizon.

Arelan turned slowly, his hand instinctively reaching for the dagger at his side. The world was still, the shadows deep, but there was something unsettling about the quiet that had settled over them. It wasn't just the aftermath of the Emperor's death, the chaos that followed. There was something more. Something... other.

"What are you hearing?" he asked, his voice low, a sharp edge of concern creeping in. He had fought beside Althea for so long, had seen her power, her strength, and yet there was something in her voice now that unsettled him.

Althea stepped closer to him, her eyes wide, the vulnerability in them raw and unguarded. "Whispers," she murmured. "Whispers beyond the veil. It feels like—like there's something watching. Something waiting."

Arelan's hand tightened on the dagger, his muscles tensing instinctively. There had been a moment, fleeting but sharp, when he had felt it too—the same unease, the same feeling that something was out of place. But he had dismissed it, focused on the fight ahead, on the people who needed them. Now, standing beside Althea, the air felt thicker, almost oppressive, as though they were not alone in this world anymore.

He reached for her hand, his fingers brushing against hers, trying to ground himself in the touch. "What do you mean, Althea? What whispers?"

Her eyes flickered toward him, but there was something distant in them, something far away, as if she were listening to a voice he couldn't hear. "I don't know," she whispered, her voice trembling. "I don't know what it is. But it's calling to me. To us. It's... something older than the Stone. Older than the Emperor. Something that has always been here, just beyond our reach."

Arelan's heart skipped a beat as he pulled her closer, his eyes scanning the dark horizon. He could feel it now, a subtle tug at the edges of his mind, a whisper that made his skin crawl. There was something in the air, something that he couldn't name, but it was as real as the dagger in his hand, as real as the world around them. It felt like a shadow, stretching across the very fabric of the earth, a presence waiting to reveal itself.

"It's too quiet," he said, his voice barely above a whisper. "This peace... it feels wrong."

Althea didn't answer immediately. She was still listening, still caught in the pull of something he couldn't comprehend. But Arelan could see it in her face—something was changing in her. The woman he had known, the one who had fought beside him, the one who had shared in their victory, was no longer the same. She had always carried a certain strength, a certain conviction, but now, there was a fragility to her, a sense of something unraveling.

"It's pulling at me, Arelan," she said, her voice barely audible. "I can feel it. It's reaching into me. I—I don't know how much longer I can hold it back."

He pulled her into him, his hand gripping her shoulder tightly, trying to ground her, trying to keep her from being lost to whatever this was. "Althea, listen to me. We've been through worse. We've beaten it before, and we can beat it again. Whatever this is, we're in this together."

She looked up at him, her eyes wide, her breath coming in short bursts. "It's not the same, Arelan. This isn't a curse. It isn't something that can be broken. It's... it's fate."

Arelan's grip tightened as he stared at her, his mind racing. Fate. The word echoed in his ears like a distant drumbeat, a relentless rhythm that pulled at the very core of him. He had never believed in fate. He had always fought against it, fought for his own freedom, for the choice to determine his own path.

But now, in this moment, with Althea trembling in his arms, he wasn't so sure.

"We choose our fate, Althea," he said, his voice fierce with the defiance that had carried them both this far. "We've always chosen it. And we'll choose it again."

But Althea shook her head, her expression strained, torn. "You don't understand. This isn't something we can fight. This… this is bigger than us. It's older than us."

Arelan could feel the cold sweat on his forehead, the weight of her words settling into the pit of his stomach. He didn't want to believe it. He didn't want to think that this—this thing that was pulling at them both—was something they couldn't defeat. Something that had always been waiting for them, just beyond the veil of their understanding.

The air around them thickened, and the whispers grew louder, until they were no longer just in Althea's mind. They were in the air, in the wind, in the very stones of the sanctuary itself. They were everywhere. Arelan could feel them now, brushing against his skin, seeping into his thoughts. They spoke in a language he couldn't understand, but their meaning was clear.

It's time. The reckoning has come. You cannot escape what is written.

The words seemed to echo in the very air, vibrating in the marrow of his bones, making his heart race. He could feel the pull now, a pressure building inside him, a force trying to push him toward something—toward the unknown.

"I'm not afraid," Althea said, her voice trembling, but there was a steel in her words now, a spark of defiance. "But I'm scared of losing you. I'm scared of what this will do to us."

Arelan swallowed hard, his chest tight. He didn't know what she was hearing, what she was feeling, but he knew that whatever this was, whatever this thing was, they couldn't fight it like they had fought the Emperor. They couldn't outlast it.

"You won't lose me, Althea," he said, his voice soft but filled with conviction. "We'll fight this together, just like we've done before. We'll find a way."

The whispers intensified, swirling around them, filling the space with a terrifying presence. The wind howled through the sanctuary, carrying with it the scent of something ancient, something beyond their comprehension. The shadows that stretched across the stone walls seemed to move, as though alive, as though they were the living remnants of something that had been waiting for centuries.

And then, from the darkness, a figure stepped forward.

It was barely a silhouette at first, its form flickering in and out of existence, but as it drew closer, Arelan's heart skipped a beat. He recognized it immediately, though it shouldn't have been possible.

The figure was human—at least in form—but its eyes gleamed

with the cold, ancient light of the shadows. The figure was tall, draped in dark robes that seemed to swallow the light around them. Its presence was overpowering, almost suffocating.

"You have broken the bonds," the figure said, its voice a low, echoing murmur that sent chills down Arelan's spine. "But you have not escaped the path laid before you. You never could."

Althea's hand shot out to grip Arelan's arm, her fingers icy cold. Her voice trembled, but there was no fear in it. Only a burning defiance. "Who are you?"

The figure's lips curled into a faint, knowing smile. "I am the one who watches. The one who waits in the spaces between the worlds. I am the gatekeeper. The harbinger of what comes next."

Arelan's mind raced as the weight of the figure's words settled over him. "What comes next?" he asked, his voice strained.

The figure's eyes gleamed. "The choice is yours. The veil has lifted. The world is yours to shape. But know this—there is no escaping what has been set into motion. You will choose your path, but the road will be long, and the cost…" It leaned forward, its voice dropping to a whisper, "…will be greater than you can imagine."

The world seemed to close in around Arelan as the figure faded back into the shadows, its voice lingering in the air, echoing in his mind.

The reckoning has come.

And in that moment, Arelan understood. The path they had chosen was just the beginning. The real fight—the fight for their future, for their love—was only about to begin.

www.ingramcontent.com/pod-product-compliance
Lightning Source LLC
LaVergne TN
LVHW011945070526
838202LV00054B/4802